D1427602

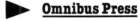 IN OTHER WORDS...DAVID BOWIE ■■

Omnibus Press
LONDON/NEW YORK/SYDNEY/COLOGNE

EDITED BY KERRY JUBY

George Underwood
Vic Furlong
Brian Lane
Ronnie Ross
Mrs Margaret Jones
Les Conn
Denis Taylor
Dana Gillespie
Ken Pitt
Lindsay Kemp
Natasha Kornilof
Angie Bowie
Mary Finnigan
Roger Raven
Ray Stevenson
Tony Visconti
Gus Dudgeon
Anthony Zanetta
Leee Childers
Mick Ronson
Carlos Alomar
Brian Eno
Nicolas Roeg
Jack Hofsiss
Julie Weiss
Louis Marks
Nile Rogers
Hugh Padgham
Sean Mayes
Julian Temple
Bhaskar Bhattachoryia

Interviews by Kerry Juby except:
Lindsay Kemp conducted by Mary Finnigan

Jack Hofsiss
Nile Rogers
Julie Weiss } conducted by Sue Woodman
Tony Zanetta
Carlos Alomar

Photographic Research
Kevin Cann

Additional Script
Mary Finnigan

Narrator
(Radio Series) Angie Bowie

Compiled and Produced
Kerry Juby

Executive Producer
(Radio Series) Tim Blackmore

Transcription
Linda Griffiths

Artwork and Design
Kevin Cann/Stuart Young – Avatar

Typeset by
Chris Quinn – Avatar

Text Editor
Chris Charlesworth

All Interviews
Copyright 1985/1986
Stage Broadcast

Thanks are extended to everyone who helped in the production of this book, from those interviewed to those helpful with its construction: John Wigham (Slidewise), Tania Jackson, Jane Doberman, Melanie Cann and Chris Quinn.

Photo Sources: Pictorial Press/Stage Broadcast/Leee Black Childers/Ray Stevenson/Kenneth Pitt/Kevin Cann/Sean Mayes/Henson Associates/BBC/Denis Taylor/Starzone Magazine (PO Box 225, Watford, Herts.)

Extracts of interviews from this book are available on a picture disc album, narrated by Angela Bowie. Catalogue No. IOW1. Available from all good record shops.

© Copyright 1986 Omnibus Press
(A Division of Book Sales Limited)

ISBN No. 0.7119.1038.3
Order No. OP 44114

Exclusive distributors:

Book Sales Limited
8/9 Frith Street, London W1V 5TZ.

Music Sales Corporation
24, East 22nd Street, New York, NY 10010, USA.

Omnibus Press
GPO Box 3304, Sydney, NSW 2001, Australia.

To the Music Trade only:

Music Sales Limited
8/9 Frith Street, London W1V 5TZ.

Printed in England by
The Anchor Press Limited, Tiptree, Essex.

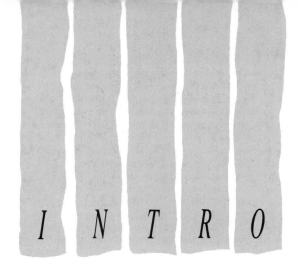

INTRO

About to board the Isle of Wight ferry, Davie Jones 1965. ▶

Elvis pout '78. ▶

◀◀
Previous page – On Stage at Live Aid, Wembley 1985.

In Other Words — David Bowie, is the story of David Bowie, documented in a diverse range of perspectives from actors, musicians, producers, directors and friends connected with his life and work. The object of the book is not to analyse but to report, which is why it is predominantly the words of others taken from the radio series that I produced, In Other Words — David Bowie, a series that was narrated by Angie, David's former wife.

This project began back in 1976 when I was working for Capital Radio, London's independent local radio station. It was at that time that I interviewed David's mother, *Margaret Jones,* who recalled a three-year-old David discovering a bag of make-up in an upstairs room and plastering himself with it, and how at one point she thought he would become a ballet dancer. For various reasons I am unable to publish a transcript of everything that was said, although some salient points are to be found in the book.

David was sacked from his very first job at *Vic Furlongs* Music Shop in Bromley; he was working there whilst still at school but, as Vic describes, "He was a day-dreamer and had to be gotten rid of."

The early years are documented by *Ronnie Ross,* his saxophone tutor, *Brian Lane,* his music teacher, and *George Underwood,* who first met David in Bromley Cubs when both were nine years old. He recalls that when other boys of David's age listened to Radio Luxemburg, David was tuned in to American football on the American Forces Network, and was fascinated not only by American music, but by the whole culture of America.

His first record was released in June 1964 when he was managed by *Les Conn,* who remembers how David and Marc Bolan would redecorate his office between gigs, and David's first television appearance when he refused to cut his hair.

Back in the early 60s, David and a group called The Lower Third would travel to gigs in an old ambulance, and *Dana Gillespie* recalls the story she heard of them "scoring" one night when the van was parked in Piccadilly Circus.

Ken Pitt, David's third manager, recalls his first flirtation with Buddhism and David's involvement with *Lindsay Kemp,* a relationship that Lindsay recalls himself. Not only was David having an affair with Kemp, but also with *Natasha Kornilof* at the same time.

At the time "Space Oddity" was written, David had moved in with *Mary Finnigan* and they launched the Beckenham Folk Club (in order to raise some money) which later became an Arts Lab. Mary recalls how they were flat broke and almost living hand to mouth. She describes how drugs were used, and how they organized a free open air festival in Beckenham Park. It was at this time that "Space Oddity" was released, a period in David's life that

brought both triumph and tragedy. *Tony Visconti* explains why, although he was making an album with David at the time, he refused to produce the "Space Oddity" single as he thought it was passé because the moon-shot was about to take place, and the lyrics "sounded like a nick from Simon and Garfunkel". *Gus Dudgeon,* who produced "Space Oddity" in the end, picks up the story.

With the Arts Lab in full swing and the free festival about to take place, David flew to Italy to take part in a song contest, the story of which is related by *Angie Bowie* and *Ken Pitt.* On his return from the song contest, his father died, and David's mother remembers how David rushed back in time to show his father the trophy he had won. Angie recalls how she moved in with David's mother to comfort her and how they eventually found Haddon Hall, a large Victorian folly in Beckenham, where ultimately she and David lived along with Tony Visconti and his girlfriend Liz.

When David revealed to the Melody Maker that he was gay, *Mick Ronson* remembers his parents' house being daubed with paint and his car being damaged — the reaction was not all good. He also tells the story of the preparations for the launch of Ziggy Stardust, with Angie describing how David's new manager, *Tony DeFries,* took over organizing the business side of things. For Pitt, it was a sad parting of the ways, and he describes the final meeting with David and Tony DeFries.

◀
Bowie's portrayal of the Elephant Man in 1980.

Tony Zanetta, former President of MainMan, the company set up by Tony DeFries to handle David's career, takes us behind the scenes and describes the setting up of MainMan. "Tony wanted an empire, he wanted an international entertainment conglomerate which was MainMan. He was very taken with organization in the corporate world, and MainMan was fashioned after a large corporation although, at least in its beginning, it was anything but that."

The rise of MainMan is also documented by *Leee Black Childers* who describes his horrendous journey with David across Russia on the Trans-Siberian Express.

In later years both Tony DeFries and Ken Pitt ended up in litigation with Bowie. As Dana Gillespie recalls, "I'm sure everyone's got a different version of it, and I really didn't witness any rows, but I would often hear from my assistant who would tell me he'd just come back from MainMan offices and the door was closed into DeFries's inner sanctum, and there were raised voices between David and him in there. I think he did say to me once that he was very disturbed at how much coke David was doing, and it got to the point where he didn't hide it in front of DeFries, whereas he did, for quite a while, at first."

Angie recalls how, in the high-flying days of MainMan, David turned to using drugs and how their marriage began to crumble. Sadly they were to part with Angie attempting suicide and David snatching their son Zowie back from Angie while she was away from her home in Switzerland. Tony Visconti tells the story of how he testified against Angie in the struggle for custody of Zowie, and how David was frequenting transvestite clubs of Berlin while making an album with Iggy Pop and Brian Eno. Eno describes David's first adventure into the world of cybernetics and the making of their trilogy of albums.

The story takes us through his films, shows, tours, from *The Man Who Fell To Earth* (about which *Nicolas Roeg* recalls, "I was asked by the company — can he act? — to which I replied — what do you mean can he act? Anyone who holds 60,000 people on their own in a hall, is an act; they don't do that at home. Their act is acting"), to *Absolute Beginners* and *Labyrinth*.

In order to make the radio series, over 30 interviews were recorded exclusively, although only 5% could be used in the finished production, which is why I decided to produce this book, which will prove to be an excellent documentation on the life of David Bowie — an insight into this enigma of the rock world — told by those who really know.

Kerry Juby, 1986.

Just A Gigolo, Berlin 1978. ▼

CONTENTS

INTRO		4
ONE	HIGH SCHOOL HIGHS	8
TWO	THE ARTS ODDITY	24
THREE	THE AMERICAN DREAM	50
FOUR	THE ACTOR'S TALE	76
FIVE	A NEW CAREER IN A NEW TOWN	92
SIX	THE BEAT GOES ON	108

HIGH SCHOOL HIGHS

O N E

Stockwell Junior School – David's Brixton Junior School as it is today. ►►

No. 40 Stansfield Road, Brixton. David's birthplace. ►

In 1946 Howard Stenton Jones set up home with Margaret Burns in Stanstead Road, Brixton, along with Terry, Margaret's son from her previous marriage.

"We had a tough time in those days," recalled **Mrs Jones,** "the post war years were no party for anyone, and we were no exception.

"David was born on 8th January (1947). The midwife said to me, *'This child has been on this earth before'* and I thought that was rather an odd thing to say, but the midwife seemed quite adamant.

"When he was about 3 years old, he put on make-up for the first time. We had tenants in the house and one day he went missing upstairs and found a bag of lipstick, eye-liner and face powder, and decided it would be a good idea to plaster his face with it. When I finally found him, he looked for all the world like a clown. I told him that he shouldn't use make-up, but he said, 'You do Mummy'. I agreed, but pointed out that it wasn't for little boys."

David was 4½ when he first went to school and not unlike most mothers, Mrs Jones was upset at not having him around the house. He proved to be independent, even at this early age. When his mother took him to school on the first day, he decided from then onwards he could make his own way to school and didn't hesitate in telling his mother just that.

At his first school, Stockwell Junior School, David dressed up for the first time in a school nativity play. Mrs Jones recalls, "I made him a robe and head-dress and his father made him a crook. He was mad about it — he absolutely loved it — it was then we began to realize that there was something in David."

In those days, there was no television, but David, according to his mother, made the most of the radio. "If there was anything that caught his ear, he would tell everyone to be quiet and listen, and then fling himself about to the music. In those days, we thought he might be a ballet dancer."

From Stockwell Junior School, David attended Burnt Ash Primary School. By now the Joneses had moved to Plaistow Grove, Sundridge Park, Bromley, a small and leafy dormitory area on the outskirts of London. It was around this time that he met George Underwood who was to become a life-long friend.

George Underwood: "I don't know what year it was — I think it was the year when Tom Hark was No. 1 (1958-Ed.) — but we went to the Isle of Wight with the 18th Bromley Scouts (we were in the Cubs then). It was a skiffle group basically. We had a double bass, tea chest/broom handle/gut and a ukulele, and we did 'Gambling Man' and 'Cumberland Gap' and a few of the old Lonnie Donegan things, and that was David's first public

appearance, on the Isle of Wight. From what I remember, we went down quite well and it was the beginning of quite an interesting career for the young Mr Jones."

In those days, most kids listened to Buddy Holly and followed football or cricket, but David was different even then. He used to listen to American Football on the American Forces Network and was so enthused with it that he wrote to the American Embassy, who invited him to visit them for the day.

George Underwood: "It was all instigated by David really, because he'd been listening to the World Service on the radio and suddenly got the bug to get involved in American football, and he wrote to the American Embassy asking for more information. They got the impression that he was well into it but, in fact, it was only about a week before that he'd started to get interested. I think it was the glamour or the aesthetics of the American football player. They made our football players look a bit weak because of all the big shoulder pads and everything. Anyway, the embassy wrote back to him asking whether he'd like to visit — I went along with him. At the end of the day, they presented David with a complete baseball outfit, padded shoulders, football helmet, which he proudly brought to school the following day. It was quite amazing really because we'd never seen any of these things before. You can just imagine this little boy in the playground, when everyone else is kicking a soccer

Bromley Tech School badge. ▼

George Underwood, David's school friend. ▼

Bromley Tech, David's secondary school. ▼

ball, dressed with big padded shoulders and a helmet and an American football — it was quite bizarre really.

"I think he was very much into the magic of America. The certain mystique it had was much more than just Cowboys and Indians on television. He had a period that he went through just reading books about America. Even at that age, he was listening to Charlie Mingus and people like that. Not that I thought he understood the music that much, but it was the image of the people behind the music, because people like Charlie Mingus are quite characters. It's quite well known that Little Richard was one of David's idols, but there's a lot of other American people who interested David, as much from the image point of view as the music."

David's step-brother, Terry, was also a great influence on David in the early years. When David was 8, Terry was 16, frequenting jazz cellars and introducing David to writers like Jack Kerouac and Allen Ginsberg.

At the age of 11, David transferred to Bromley Technical High School. Although he'd passed his 11 plus, he chose to go to a technical school as it would be more art orientated.

George Underwood: "I remember when we were at Bromley Tech, we would experiment with telepathy. We would arrange to be something at a particular time in the evening and then the following day we would compare our thoughts. It was uncanny how on so many occasions, our thoughts were similar."

Brian Lane (schoolteacher): "One thing I remember about David was something that he didn't take part in, which was a concert held at the school in aid of a pavilion that was being put up by the parents and teachers, and being paid for by them. So popular was this concert that there was no admission charge, only a collection, as it went on for two evenings, but strangely enough, David didn't offer to take part, although George Underwood did and he had a very popular group called George and The Dragons at the time. However, later David did come and see me to ask if his group could play on the school steps at the PTA fête which was to be held in the summer, so I suppose that was one of his first public engagements with his group. He was delighted to have the opportunity to do it. I also recall that at least on one or two occasions, he dyed his hair which was almost unheard of in the early 60s. However, some way or other, it was always washed out the next day and back to normal."

In common with most teenagers, David took a couple of part-time jobs, one riding around on a pushbike with a basket on the front for a butcher, and another working for a record shop owned by Vic Furlong.

George Underwood: "I remember how we used to hang around on Saturday listening to records. We'd never buy anything. In fact it was from Vic Furlong's shop that David bought his first saxophone. He couldn't play it at the time, but it made some really great noises. When he saw the saxophone, he told his father about it and his father said that if he could save half the money, he would make up the other half."

Vic Furlong: "He was always a bit of a dreamer in that I'd give him a job to do, come back in about an hour and he was still chatting, the job unfinished, so he had to go. He was a nice enough lad. In fact, at the time, I was involved with Bromley Theatre, and as some of his interest lay in this field, he wanted me to arrange an introduction. But he was a bit of a dreamer — so he had to go."

▲
The Kon-Rads rock it up in South London.

Having acquired his first saxophone, David got in touch with the jazz saxophonist, *Ronnie Ross,* after finding his telephone number in the 'phone book.

Ronnie Ross: "At the time he came to me for lessons, groups like The Rolling Stones were just beginning to come into vogue although he was more interested in jazz, and we'd sit and talk about jazz and jazz musicians quite often. He didn't talk about groups he was involved with but I did know he was playing with a group. He was quite an average sort of pupil, nothing out of the ordinary, and I certainly didn't expect him to become what he is today."

George Underwood: "We had periods when we would bring a guitar into school, particularly when it was raining. It was what you called a 'wet break' and you weren't allowed to go outside. There was a stairway leading from our form room which had good acoustics and we'd sit there on the steps, and I'd be playing guitar and David would be singing. We did Buddy Holly stuff and Everly Brothers. He was a good harmonizer and still is. He was studying to be a commercial artist and when he was in Mr Frampton's art class (this was Peter Frampton's father) in his later years at Bromley Tech, Frampton lectured the form on how he would not tolerate tapered trousers."

Margaret Jones: "I remember David asked me to get my dressmaker to taper his trousers and before long other members of his form were also getting me to taper their trousers, so I suppose in a way I was almost helping them to rebel against Mr Frampton."

George Underwood: "When you leave school, you have to queue up and see a careers officer and I remember I was standing right behind David in the queue and asked him what sort of job he was going to say he was looking for. 'A saxophonist in a modern jazz quartet' came the reply. The careers officer offered him a job in a harp factory in Bromley!"

David left school with 2 GCE 'O' level passes, in art and woodwork, and the school found him a job as a junior with a commercial art company, The Design Group Ltd., and although some early press releases said that David was expelled from school, the record shows that he left two or three days early to start the job.

Davie Jones, 1965. ▲

Margaret Jones: "He only took the job for his father's sake because his father thought that all this business with groups and music could well be a passing fad and that at least if he spent a year or so at work, it would give him some stable grounding to fall back on. So David did go to work there, though not without protest. I can remember him coming home and moaning about his 'blooming job' and travelling up and down on the train."

It was 1963 and as David started his new job, 'Mersey Mania' was taking its stranglehold on the charts with The Beatles, Gerry and The Pacemakers, Freddie and The Dreamers; everything with a Liverpudlian accent tasted success. Soon David left his job and, along with George Underwood, formed a band called *The King Bees*.

George Underwood: "David was always a bit over the top and he decided to write to John Bloom, a millionaire businessman, saying something to the effect 'Brian Epstein has got The Beatles but you can have us', but Bloom wasn't that interested and passed his letter to Les Conn, an agent."

Les Conn: "The problem was John (Bloom) didn't know anybody in the music business except myself, because I was quite well-known at the time in Tin Pan Alley. Bloom got on to me and said he had received a letter from this young, cheeky so-and-so and to give him an audition and see what he was like — which I did — and was quite impressed. I got in touch with Bloom and said that I thought the guy had talent and Bloom told me that he was having a wedding anniversary party in Soho, which is in the centre of London, and to give the group £20 and see what he was like. 'You cheap-skate' I said, 'What sort of millionaire are you? You could at least give them about £100 to pay for their expenses'.

Anyway, at the party, there was the aristocracy of the land and quite a lot of celebrities and of course, David and his group turned up in scruffy jeans."

George Underwood: "When we arrived, everyone was rather dressed up and we wore jeans, we were rather shabby looking and got some funny looks. The first number we did was 'I've Got My Mojo Working' and the people in there weren't quite sure what was going on. We didn't exactly get the bird but they just couldn't handle it — they didn't know what sort of music we were playing. We were pretty much trying to emulate a lot of the early black blues sound. With my guitar, I was trying to sound like Lightning Hopkins and John Lee Hooker and people like this, and we just thought '. . . this sounds OK', and it didn't sound too bad at the time. So we were doing this music which was away from the pop stuff that was around. Now 'I've Got My Mojo Working' doesn't go down with everyone but at that time, there were a few people around who did like that kind of stuff, and we were hopefully appealing to them."

Les Conn: "Well, of course, the people weren't prepared for that kind of entertainment and they all put their hands over their ears, and Bloom started screaming, 'Get them off, they're ruining my wedding party'. So, when they'd finished performing 'I've Got My Mojo Working,' I pointed out to David that these people didn't really appreciate the music and David, being the sensitive soul that he was, burst into tears. I told him not to worry and that I was quite impressed and would be interested in managing the band. That's how it began.

"I used to get them various gigs at the Marquee Club in Wardour Street and the Roundhouse, and some dates at universities throughout the country, but there wasn't an awful lot coming in although I did succeed in getting him a TV appearance and the producer, who was a good friend of mine, said, 'I'll not have this guy on my programme with long hair'."

Dana Gillespie: "This was about the time The Beatles were just starting and they were considered to have long hair, but if you look at the pictures of them in those days, they had almost crew-cuts compared to David's which was honestly long, bright yellow, bleached blonde from a bottle. He was an extraordinary sight. In fact, I remember when I first introduced him to my father and before he'd said a word, I said, 'This is my father' who told me afterwards that he hadn't realized that it was a boy because I mean . . . long hair — his hair was really long."

Les Conn: "So anyway, I said to David, 'I think you'll have to have your hair cut, otherwise you won't get this programme on television', to which he told me that he wouldn't cut his hair for the Prime Minister. It was then that I conceived the idea of getting the few fans that he had in those days to walk around the television company with placards saying 'Let's be Fair to the Long Hairs', which did get press

publicity, and in the end the producer relented and he did his first TV show."

Daily Mirror: "Davie, who comes from Bromley in Kent, said 'I have no intention of having my hair cut. Mr Langford has left the matter open until Friday in case I change my mind, but I won't'. Mr Langford, 39, said, 'Kids today just don't want this long hair business any more'."

Les Conn: "By this time, I had arranged a recording test with Decca and David had his first single released called 'Liza Jane' which was on Vocalion."

Dana Gillespie: "Actually, before the first single came out, he was doing a support act at The Marquee. I can't remember who he was supporting, but I was a regular visitor because being a big blues fan, it meant I could go and see Sonny Boy Williamson, and all the people who would be at the Richmond Jazz/American Blues Folk Festival that came every year. So I was down there watching The

Yardbirds and the English bands that were starting, and one time there was this band — for some reason I was there early and watching the sound check — with this blond guy who had very long blond hair, and knee length sort of suede, fringed, Sherwood Forest, Robin Hood looking boots, playing a bit of sax on stage. In the break before he actually started, I was standing at the mirror brushing my hair and he came up, took the brush out of my hand — I had very long, waist length peroxide blonde hair in those days — and he said, *'What are you doing after the show?'* He just chatted me up. In fact, I used to see him quite regularly as a boyfriend. He'd walk me home from school and it's often said that he carried my ballet shoes, which sounds kind of romantic, but he actually did sometimes, if I was carrying a whole load of things. He'd meet me from school — I was at drama school then.

"In those days, I used to hang out at the Giaconda Cafe in Denmark Street where all broke musicians hang out, and I remember his first single came out and he dragged me into the record store next door, Francis Day & Hunter, and said 'Have a listen to this'. And then we bought a copy of the New Musical Express and saw the little ad that went with it. They were quite good days because I knew absolutely nothing about the music business, being at school, and he was my first boyfriend who wasn't upper-class. I had no idea there was a class distinction, having lived in a sort of world of my own, and when I went to meet his parents in his house in Bromley, I'd never been to such a small, little house where all the chairs had those things on the back where you catch the Brylcreem and you sat down and had high tea. It was a kind of life-style I knew nothing about, having always lived in South Kensington. People that I have known through the years in the music business always knew where to find me and I never moved address. My parents lived in the big house and I built a studio and had a whole little place where I could live in the basement and it was very convenient, so David would come round there."

Les Conn: "Anyway, at the time, I thought 'This is ridiculous, I'm holding these boys back' because I was also managing a singer called Marc Bolan, and in the quieter moments, he and David would deco-

◄ *Phil Lancaster, Davie Jones and friends, 1966.*

The original 'Lower Third Mobile', 1965. ▼

On stage at the Marquee for the 'Inecto' radio shows. ▶

rate my office to fill in the time, but I said to them that I had just run out of money and couldn't afford to carry on — I'd taken no commission from either of them at the time — so I went off to Spain to think about my next move and released them both from their contracts."

By this time, The King Bees had released a second single but this time without David Jones, although George Underwood was still with the band. David had moved from The King Bees to *The Manish Boys* and released a single 'I Pity the Fool', and having supported Gerry and the Pacemakers, The Kinks and Gene Pitney on tour, joined up with a group called *The Lower Third,* consisting of *Graham Rivens, Phil Lancaster and Denis Taylor.*

Denis Taylor: "We decided we were going to have a new singer and hold auditions, the idea being that we would go to the old club we used to play in called La Discothèque, which was in Wardour Street, not far from the Whiskey-a-GoGo. The manager let us have it because he knew us. Anyway, Davy came along and Steve Marriot also came along on that day, because quite a few people heard about it, as we put the word out at the Giaconda Cafe in Denmark Street. Anyway, David was terrific and we all made our decision in the Giaconda, and that's how it all really started.

"We liked the stuff he was doing and he really started to develop an image for us as well. We were quite long haired — sort of early Rolling Stones type. I think he was coming to the end of his management with Les Conn at the time. He was a nice person and I think he was genuinely interested in how David was getting on although he couldn't get him any bookings. David was ambitious for all of us —

he was honestly ambitious for all of us and we loved it. He became a driving force. He'd come to us with numbers he wanted to get off and I'd just play a chord on the guitar and he'd write a number round it. He was the one that did all the pushing because he knew the business. He wrote this little publicity thing under the name *'Truth Shows'* and sent it to various places, and one of the places he sent it to was Happy Towers in Edgbaston in Birmingham, which was a Mecca ballroom, and that was the first gig we did, complete with a revolving stage and everything. We barely knew any numbers at all at that time, but we got away with noise and after that we fast became the second loudest group in London playing gigs at Brighton, Hastings, Birmingham, Newcastle, Tadcaster. In fact, it was coming back from the Tadcaster job that the old Atlas van that we had blew up — the big ends just blew out of it and we had to dump it there and go.

"'Liza Jane' and 'I Pity the Fool' were released at the time we joined him because he brought this record along and said 'What do you think of this?' We were obviously impressed because he'd got a record released. Anyway, it didn't get anywhere and the first record we released with David was 'You've Got A Habit Of Leaving', which we did at IBM Studios in Portland Street. Just as the record was going to be released, Dave came round and told us he'd got another manager for us and it turned out to be *Ralph Horton,* who we auditioned for at The Roebuck Pub in Tottenham Court Road. We were up on the top floor and Ralph Horton came up to listen to us and was impressed, although I think he was more impressed with David than us. He was a queen, incidentally. He had a boyfriend called

Neil Andersen who was German I think, really blonde hair. He was quite tall and very handsome, and I guess he was his assistant. Anyway, he took a liking to David definitely, and from that point it was no longer a singer and a group, it had become a singer with a group, which is a different thing altogether. When we went to gigs, David used to travel in Ralph Horton's car and we used to have to go in the old ambulance which replaced the old Atlas van. It was Graham who bought the old ambulance, not David. Graham's father actually gave him the money to buy it from Brixton, after we'd been there to see it. Anyway, David used to travel in Ralph's Mark 10 Jag to any gigs and never used to put any of the gear away when we'd done our work, whereas before he used to. It was becoming obvious to us that Ralph was looking after David and we got hardly any money from the gigs. Poor Graham and myself were really starving and not paying the rent, and David really started looking after himself. I think he really thought he was going to get somewhere with Ralph. Mind you, Ralph did go the whole hog with it; he got Gaby Sturmer as PR doing photographs and write-ups and turned out some lovely leaflets.

"I remember one particular night, the ambulance was parked in Warwick Square where Ralph lived — it was only about 50 yards from his flat and I was really cold. It was horrible. I was trying to get myself comfortable on these padded seat things and had a blanket over me. I thought, 'What the hell am I doing here when Ralph's flat is over there? I'll go and sleep on his sofa in the lounge.' So I went over to knock on the door. There was another fellow living at Ralph's at that time called Kenny Bell who said, 'I'm sorry, you can't come in'. I was amazed. I then realized what David was doing. To me, he was bettering his career, because before that, we all worked as a team. At every gig we went to, there was a woman there — that's what we wanted, we liked to see women hanging around the star attraction of the group because he was good looking and he did stand out and look good on stage. That's the quickest way to get a name isn't it? Have groupies around. Davie always seemed to have the best girls, and none of them seemed to complain.

"By this time, my whole opinion of him changed. Instead of him being a mate, I loathed him after that until I got used to the idea. You do eventually get used to the idea. I know Graham wasn't too happy. I remember I went back to the ambulance feeling quite horrified. I thought 'Good God — it's the end of the group' — which it wasn't until a few months later.

"All this publicity we were getting was not getting us work. It only got us the £15 at the Marquee for doing a show for Radio London, the old pirate radio station. We used to do the live show that was never broadcast — it was just the bit after all the other stars have been on stage and mimed to their records for the audience. Anyway, that particular gig we did every Saturday morning. It was for £15 between four of us. Of course, Ralph would want his bit out of that as well, so obviously we weren't getting enough to pay for the rent and food, which Graham and myself desperately needed.

"We had three gigs on the trot, including The Marquee. We had Stevenage Town Hall on the Friday, The Marquee on the Saturday morning and Saturday evening we had the Brummel Club in Bromley which was David's home town at that time — we'd received a hell of a lot of publicity for that one. Anyway, at Stevenage Town Hall we told Ralph that we expected some money for these. He

said 'No way — it's got to go into publicity'. I told him that we were not eating and that we weren't paying the rent — almost destitute. He said 'No, sorry' to which we replied that we couldn't continue to play or back David if we weren't going to get any money. He just said 'It's up to you'.

"We went down to The Marquee the following morning and I think Ralph came to us and said that we could have the money for all the gigs, including The Brummel Club but after that we were finished. At The Marquee Phil's father said that Ralph was using us — he just wanted us to play tonight and then it was all over, we're finished, so why didn't we finish now? At The Brummel Club that evening, Ralph hadn't changed his mind — he said exactly the same thing — after tonight's gig you're finished. So we told him that we weren't interested in tonight's gig and that we'd take the money and go now. So we took the money for the two gigs and left them there. I remember David started crying but Ralph would not back down and say we deserved the money, or to have some of it, so we just left them at The Brummel Club before doing their thing.

On the Isle of Wight ferry, 1965.
▼

I don't know what happened at that particular gig but I know it was his home town — it was the most important gig to David because it was in front of a home crowd. But during the whole thing, David never stuck up for us — that's what really got me. The last I heard of Ralph Horton was when Dave chucked him and went with Ken Pitt."

Ken Pitt: "I have a very clear memory of first meeting David. It was in 1966 at The Marquee. I went down there one Sunday afternoon to see him working. He had a series of Sunday shows down there called the Bowie Show Boat and this was the second one. I remember standing at the back of the club and just leaning against the wall and watching him. It's very difficult to put a finger on what it was that attracted me about him. I think first of all it was his amazing confidence and great personality. He had a tight hold on the audience, totally in command of his band. I like the material he was doing — not all of it was his own incidentally — but particularly, I like the way he used his entire body. There was an eloquence about his hand movements and I realized also that he could be a dancer if he wanted to be. I think these things were not common in those days and I was looking for someone who had great potential, and decided I'd found it in David Bowie.

"He'd been making some records but they weren't successful and for the first few weeks after I'd met him and decided to work with him, I was listening to songs that he'd written, and was in the process of writing, and came to the conclusion that he was not essentially a singles artist. The sort of material he was writing and playing, to me, was album stuff. Now in those days, you never got an album deal from a record company unless you had a hit single, but I made up my mind that the sort of stuff he had would make a very good album, so I went to Decca with that view in mind, trying to get him an album deal, and did get a deal for him. That's how we did our first album which was on the Decca label called 'David Bowie'.

"One of my old friends at Decca was a man called Hugh Mendl and he was in charge of the singles department. I played a couple of tracks to Hugh and he liked them very much and wanted to hear some more, so I took some more up to him. It so happened that Hugh was the man who had been producing Tony Newley and he said to me after listening to those tracks that this was the most exciting thing to come into the room since Tony Newley, which I thought was amazing since, some time later, David was quite infatuated with the work of Newley. I think if you saw what David did afterwards, he was obviously attracted to the one-man show that Tony Newley was doing at the time like 'Stop the World' and things like that, and the lyrics appealed to him. He was so carried away with Newley that I believe quite unconsciously, Newley crept into Bowie's voice and, as you know, he's been accused of copying Tony Newley, but I don't think he was really aware of what he was doing at that time. The album was produced by Mike Vernon and the engineer was Gus Dudgeon."

Gus Dudgeon: "I hadn't heard of the guy before. The thing I remember about him as an engineer was that we used to get these forms that told you each week who you were going to be working on, what the line-up was, and I saw this thing and it said David Bowie, Studio Two, producer Mike Vernon, Gus Dudgeon, blah, blah, and this weird list of instruments like bass flute, contra bassoon, bass drum, etc., and I thought this was very peculiar, but it was the early days of the Deram label and we used to do some pretty odd sessions. So this guy came in, and he was just extraordinary. He was obviously way ahead of his time. He had a completely different way of doing anything from anybody else. Whatever the rules were, they were not necessarily made to be broken, but they weren't necessarily there to be obeyed either. He had a great attitude about him. He was right at the height of his Anthony Newley hang-up, so one problem was constantly reminding him that he sounded like Anthony Newley and trying to 'de-Newleyfy' him if you could.

"I remember people coming in from funny countries — you know, Turkish people and Indian people, and Americans coming in to play oboe. I don't know where he got them all from but it was always very interesting, and we worked our way through an album that was subsequently released. I must admit I really enjoyed working with him and we did tracks like 'The Laughing Gnome' and I have to say, I am one of the gnomes on that record and am responsible for some of the terrible jokes on it as well. So we 'gnomed' it for a while. Then we did

things like 'Love You 'Till Tuesday' which we did with a huge orchestra, as I recall, which was done in another studio. After the album, we did two or three scattered tracks and various things, but as none of it really sold, we suddenly didn't see him around any more. That was my first experience with him basically."

Ken Pitt: "But the big value of that album was that it brought David's work to the attention of a lot of very important people. I remember I bought about 100 copies of it and sent it to various agents, bookers and media. One of them, in actual fact, got into the hands of *Lindsay Kemp* and Lindsay used to use the album as background for his mime work at his concerts. David heard about that, went along to see it one day, and that's how the partnership with Lindsay started."

Lindsay Kemp: "It had been arranged through NEMS' office that we should meet. I'd heard the voice of an angel — and when a meeting was eventually arranged between David and myself, through NEMS' who were handling both of us at the time, I expected a very pimply youth to be standing there. However, when I opened the blue painted door at Bateman's building, there in fact, was angel. Love at first sight. It had already been love at first hearing. Bowie and I immediately, from that moment standing in the doorway, hit it off. We began work immediately. He chose me as his master, which appealed to me enormously, as it's one of my functions in life to be a teacher, so I was very happy at being his kind of pedagogue.

"We began to prepare a show which became Pierrot In Turquoise — turquoise because it's the British symbol of everlastingness and David claims that I saved him — not from Buddhism, not from everlastingness, but from becoming a Tibetan monk. I do remember saying 'Look, you can give yourself to God but to me as well, and the public. You don't have to leave any of us out. You can be a marvellous entertainer. You know the entertainer first gives himself to God and then the public.' I just gave him something on the side. I didn't really teach him to be a mime artiste but to be more of himself physically on the outside. My endeavour as a teacher really is to make people more of what I believe they are inside. I enabled him to free the angel and the demon that he is on the inside. It helped him to dance, but for me to dance is a way of allowing and encouraging ourselves to escape through our fingertips, eyelids, lungs and tips of tongues. He already did it with his tongue, but up to that period his fingers were a bit stiff. Mine had been a decade earlier when Marcel Marceau removed my hands from behind my back; hands, which at that period didn't resemble hands at all, but strawberry coloured boxing gloves. Marcel gave me my hands and a generation later, I gave David Bowie his wings.

"When we first met, there was a great deal of affection — there was a great deal of love and a great deal of admiration and respect as well you know. I think that when love, and emotion, and passion, and sexual passion are mixed with respect, then that's the most ideal kind of relationship for me. We weren't lovers from the beginning — it took about 30 seconds.

"As a pupil he was marvellous, immediately responsive, especially when he was there. Of course, he wasn't always there because frequently there were notes from his mother to say that he had earache or something, but later on I realized, of course, that those notes had been faked, the same as the notes that I had sent to school from my mother

◄ *David's mime teacher, Lindsay Kemp.*

Mime shot by David's old manager, Kenneth Pitt.
◄

Plaistow Grove, Bromley (with white wall). ▼

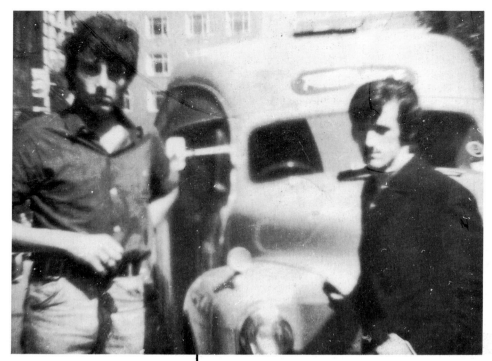

The famous Lower Third ▲
ambulance. Left to right, Graham Rivens and Denis 'T-Cup' Taylor.

David on the consumer trail, London '66. ▶

several generations before that. But I was fooled, like we always are when we're in love — blinded you know. Then, of course, he'd send his other friends similar notes — can't stay tonight, got terrible earache, or my mother's not very well — because, for something like a year or more, he was having a double affair with — dare I mention her name — *Natasha Kornilof,* who was a great friend of mine. Of course, she had no idea."

Natasha Kornilof: "I have to say David never gave me any notes. I don't question people very hard about where they've been. I always take at face value what they say to me. I'm fairly naïve about it. I never had any notes. If Lindsay had notes — well tough — it's because he doesn't believe as readily as I do what people say to me. If they don't over-elaborate the story I don't question it. It's when they tell you more and more of a story — that's when you disbelieve.

"Yes, this now celebrated affair, which I've not spoken about before, did actually happen. He did give everybody the run-around, but was wonderfully attractive and, indeed, still is. It's not surprising is it? He's very beautiful and very loving and a very great pleasure to be with. What more can one say?

"Lindsay always gave him hell. Said he was as stiff as a ramrod and would get nowhere, but he's pretty hard on people anyway. But, Lindsay is also a very great teacher. He's taught an awful lot of people, including myself, an awful lot of things. Before Lindsay, I made costumes — after Lindsay, I made magic. That's what I owe to him. I benefited amazingly from the experience and I think almost anybody who has ever worked with Lindsay has benefited from the experience. It really is something, though he is hard on you and he is difficult.

"David had a couple of records out at the time and he sang all his songs in the show that we did. We toured the show — I was designer/driver. We got a dreadful van from a man called Nick the Maltese, down the East End. I'd never driven a van in my life but I managed to drive it from the East End to the West End, which I found a feat, and then I finally drove it up to Cumberland in the snow which was even more of a feat. We were like a terrible gypsy encampment. We arrived and stayed at a farm house

with these people in Cumberland. It was all extraordinarily unreal, this tour we did.

"Lindsay was Pierrot basically, and the show revolved around him as Pierrot. He did his various pieces of mime which were set pieces. Some he'd learnt off the Frenchman — whose name is such a household name it escapes me — Marcel Marceau — and Jack Birkett (now known as The Great Orlando) was Harlequin, who could also be Columbine. It was quite wonderful. I made Jack shave his head — because he had the remnants of his hair hanging on — wonderful shape of a head — shave that off. I put him in drag with a bare head. It was quite amazing.

"David was a character known as Cloud I think. I dressed him in this huge pink shirt with maroon spots on, with a big maroon and pink ruff and little knee britches in grey with red velvet stripes on them. Wonderful! Absolutely beautiful!

"He sang the songs that related quite indirectly to the next mime that took place and there was a slight story linking the whole thing — very slight harlequinade story — but it hardly mattered at all. Basically it was the songs and a sort of mime play with Jack, Lindsay and David leading into a set piece with Lindsay as the old woman feeding the birds, which is a wonderful one, where the bird grows and grows to a monstrous size and finally devours the old lady.

"I can't remember which of David's songs led into that — I shudder to think — but there was another lovely one about a little coat — sell me a coat because I feel cold.

"There was Lindsay like this little tremulous Pierrot (because Lindsay was very little at the time — much thinner) in these little white tights, and the coat which was like a little 18th century golden coat

18

came down from the flies, if we were lucky enough to have any up there. Some of the places were extraordinary that we played. Then he put this on and he instantly transformed into another character who did a mime to a piece of Baroque music. He was doing a little minuet and he starts finding out things about his body. He ends up doing surgery on himself and takes his heart out, listens to it like a clock and throws it to the audience. It was a wonderful piece. Very bizarre.

"It was amazingly successful. Everybody said it was magic. I even did the scenery for that one. I painted this wonderful front cloth for it — God knows where it's gone to since — I painted it on my sitting room floor with David's help. He came and helped me lay it all in which was very nice.

"The show went into penury I think. There were more and more debtors calling at Lindsay's door. It was like something from a restoration comedy as he crouched in his flat in Bateman Street and they began beating down the door. All these bills and demands.

"I can remember sitting there one whole afternoon with him while he had flu or something, and these people beating down the door. I was trying to make a list of what he owed and how we might get out of this state, which I don't think he ever got out of. I think he got out of the flat first and not out of the debt.

"He was hard on David but David certainly was talented. It was not until a few years later that I think his talent really started to manifest itself because you couldn't quite think where it was going. They were very fey little songs and they were very pleasant, but they were not earth shaking. It was only when he began having fantasies about space men that he was really in there with the hit. At that time, nobody wanted to sing about space men did they? But, as we can now see, it was like being a science fiction writer really. That's been his main stock in trade I suppose — he's always just ahead with what he says."

Lindsay Kemp: "David Bowie struck me from the very beginning as being very versatile and very 'up-front', and not in the least bit naïve. He already seemed to know a hell of a lot and taught me a lot about living, philosophy and about music. It was an exchange — for me it has to be. There's no such thing as a love affair unless there is an exchange. When I talk about love affairs, I also include platonic love affairs. I also include the love affair that I have with the public each and every night. For me, as a lover, as a person, as a man, it's not enough for me only to give — I want it back as well. In other words, I want to be loved. It's this marvellous giving and taking and sharing which provides these marvellous explosions which we call inspired moments which sometimes result in a work of art. Pierrot In Turquoise — our first child — came.

"Whilst David was continuing his studies with me, I was teaching at the Dance Centre in Covent Garden, which is an agency. Every day, I always used to stick my head around the office door and say, 'Anything for me today?' — and one day they said, 'Well, we're looking for dancers for the BBC's production of Pistol Shot (which was a play by Chekhov) — maybe you'd like to do it and choreograph it and use some of your students'. I took David Bowie and one or two of the other students to the BBC and we did it. *Hermione Farthingale* was one of the girls who had already been chosen and foolishly, I realized later, or maybe wisely, I partnered David and Hermione together because Hermione was extremely beautiful. That

wasn't the reason I gave her to David, but because she was a trained dancer and I thought she could help David get the simple steps of the minuet together, because he had difficulty in putting two steps together. Anyway, afterwards they chatted over tea in the BBC canteen, and then he escorted her towards Shepherds Bush tube station, just turning his head over his shoulder towards me. I was, of course, trailing behind about 10 paces sulking. 'I'll give you a ring later,' he said, and with Hermione Farthingale, David Bowie just walked out of my life.

"She was an English rose and extremely beautiful. I liked her immensely. She was tall and pale with ravishingly red hair. I couldn't believe that anybody could love me and a lady equally although I've had a lot of experiences since and I've known a lot of men and a lot of women since who have loved both sexes. I only wish I could do that. It would probably add to the complications of my life but it would probably lessen the hours that I have on my own, though God knows, I don't do too badly. She and I were always friends, and David and I remain friends. He'd already stabbed me in the heart several times before that with other ladies, but at least this time, there was a lady that I liked immensely. I mean, if he'd gone off with a humped back, three legged dwarf I would have felt pretty unattractive.

"I tried to interest both David and Hermione in coming up to Scotland where I lived and to play, would you believe, in 'Puss In Boots'. It was terribly naïve of me. By the time I'd asked him to come and play, he was already becoming a name in the pop music field. 'I can't' he said, 'But how much are you offering?' 'It's gone up since last time,' I replied. When we performed at The Intimate in Palmers Green, he was paid £7.10 and at The Mercury Theatre in Notting Hill Gate, I think he was paid about £4. But anyway, I said we could pay something like £25 a week, but by then Ken Pitt was finally getting him things. I remember the periods that he went through dish washing and doing house work and those kinds of things. But anyway, he and Hermione turned it down."

Having met Hermione Farthingale, David lived with her for a year. It was during this period that he

◄
The 'Ace Face' in '66.

formed a mixed media trio called *Feathers* comprising himself, Hermione and *John Hutchinson* who came from Hull. The mixed media trio did not prove successful but during that period of David's life he found work as an extra on the film *The Virgin Soldiers* and appeared in a pilot television commercial for Lyons Maid, advertising their new ice cream. It wasn't long before Hermione left Feathers, leaving just David and John Hutchinson.

Angie Bowie: "I actually met David for the first time when he was with Feathers at the Roundhouse and I was with the European head of Mercury Records, a gentleman called Lou Reisner. I met Hermione and David and John Hutchinson, who was the guitarist, at a show which was with The Scaffold and The Who. During that period, I spent a lot of time with Calvin Mark Lee, basically because he was Lou Reisner's assistant, and he and I got on really well. We used to like to go to clubs and I didn't like going by myself and Calvin was a great escort. He was great fun and loved Chinese food, which I adored, so we knew all the Chinatown speciality restaurants. It was him that arranged for David and I to meet. This was after David had split up with Hermione and was nursing a broken heart. Anyway, we went out to dinner and then went to the Speakeasy. King Crimson was being partied by a signing label and they got up and played with Donovan. It was fabulous because King Crimson had such a tremendous sound and such a tremendous image that for them to suddenly stand up and do a lot of Buddy Holly hits with Donovan singing vocals was really cute. It was a fabulous night.

Recording for 'Ready Steady Go', David Bowie and the Buzz. ▶▶
▼

"David asked if I could jive and at this particular time I always dressed as a man, which was probably another reason that Calvin and I got along very well, because Calvin wore velvet suits and I wore velvet suits — so that was one area we got on very well. But anyway, we jumped to it and started to jive and I decided that we were quite sympathetic and we got along quite well — a similar sense of humour, and lude attitude towards women — we just basically got along well.

"At the time I couldn't work legally in England and I had about two or three months to deliver my thesis for my degree. I was going out with this guy called John Colley whose relations were sort of minor gangsters in London and I went to work for them because they didn't mind my not being English.

"David and I went to the travel agency where I was working a couple of times and kept saying, 'What are you doing here?' There was a travel agency in the foyer as you came in and a girl called Dinxie and I ran this travel agency that was open during licensing hours. So, of course, what happened was that you had all these wonderful posters about as you walked in the foyer and as the punters came out drunk, you sold them weekends in Ibiza. It was all quite sensible but a little nefarious.

"It was quite rough at times — and on one occasion, I found a body outside. I called the police and was then told that I was not required to work there any longer. By this time David had started up the Arts Lab and asked me if I would teach street theatre and improvisation there, so I was destined to go to Beckenham."

Ready ... GO!

DAVIE CHANGES HIS

THE ROMNEY CONTRASTS'

DANCING in the CAVE

GRAND HOTEL, LITTLESTONE

presenting

THE LOWER THIRD

SHEERNESS CONSERVATIVE CLUB

Lower Third

SATURDAY, 10th APRIL, 1965

8.00 p.m. — 11.30 p.m.

SHEERNESS CONSERVATIVE CLUB

LOWER THIRD

on SATURDAY, 17th OCTOBER, 1964

8.00 p.m. to 11.30 p.m.

MINSTER WORKING MEN'S CLUB

DANCE

LOWER THIRD
Thursday, 8th April,

8 p.m. to 11 p.m.

...AY, 17th.   8 to 11.30 p.m.

Admi...   ...e door

BOXING DAY
with Bubbles and the Outriggers
open 7 p.m. - 7 a.m.

NEW YEAR'S EVE
with Le Grant and The Capitals
WITH MANY OTHER GUESTS TO PLAY THE OLD YEAR
OUT AND NEW IN.
OPEN AT 7 p.m.   CLOSE AT 7 a.m.

LA DISCOTHEQUE

Make ...

IE AVENGERS

RUVVER!

23rd

THE ARTS ODDITY

T W O

David in his bedroom at Kenneth Pitt's Manchester Street home. The night before his haircut for the 'Virgin Soldiers'. ▶▶

It was 1968. David was now with his third manager, Ken Pitt. Nine singles and one album had been released, but success still eluded him. He had been involved with Buddhism to the point of almost becoming a monk, and had formed the mixed media troupe called Feathers, after studying mime under Lindsay Kemp. But Feathers was to split when Hermione Farthingale decided she did not wish to continue with the group. It was at this point that David met Mary Finnigan, a journalist living in Beckenham, for the first time.

Mary Finnigan: "I first met David in the summer of 1968 when I was living with my two children in a ground floor flat in an old house in Beckenham. My top floor neighbours were a couple called Christina and Barry Jackson, and Barry had been to school with David and George Underwood in Bromley, and being a neighbour, I was quite friendly with these two. We used to socialize together and they used my garden as their flat didn't have one. It was a generally free sort of relationship.

"It was a warm spring morning and I was lying in the garden, reflecting on life in general and taking it easy, when I heard this music coming from the top floor flat where the windows were all open — and there was a somebody singing. The thing that attracted me was that it wasn't your average plonk, plonk, three chord amateur musician. It sounded extremely good, so I, lying on my back in the sunshine, shouted up to the open windows, 'Hello, who's playing that?' At this point, a rather anaemic looking face with a halo of rather greasy looking blonde curls, poked its head out of the window, looked down on me lying flat on my back and said, 'It's me, who are you?' I said, 'I'm Mary, come down and have a cup of coffee'. So, Barry, Christina and David came down and we had coffee in the sunshine, and that was the start of it basically.

"It was a couple of days later that I was alone in my flat in the evening and there was a knock on the door. I went to the door and opened it and there were about 10 people with an assortment of musical instruments — quite merry on this and that. They asked to come in, announcing themselves as an instant party. David was amongst them, and George Underwood as well. At that stage, I think David was actually just crashing around. He would spend an odd night here and an odd night there, ostensibly living with his parents. He had recently split up with Hermione and was suffering from bruised emotions and in a way, was very much alone in the world, not to mention totally penniless — he didn't have two beans to rub together. He was doing a bit of odd work here and there on an ad hoc basis, not musical work. He was working in Legastat which was a photocopying office in London and when he needed the money, he'd go and do odd bits and pieces for them, but was not very happy with his

circumstances.

"Anyway, they all came in and we had this instant party which was very pleasant. A couple of days later on, he came to visit me again, this time by himself. He sat on a stool in my kitchen while I was cooking lunch and said, 'Do you like this song?' and proceeded to play 'Space Oddity'. He had his little stylophone with him and played both parts, because 'Space Oddity' was originally written as a duet for him and Hutch who was his partner in Feathers the mixed media group, and when David split with Hermione, he and Hutch were working as a duet.

"'Space Oddity' was written as a two part song and I recall he played this song in my tiny little kitchen in Beckenham and it sounded absolutely wonderful to me."

Ken Pitt: "It was 1968 and David and I were going across to Germany quite often to do television shows and on one occasion, the producer whose name was Gunther Schneider, asked us if David would be interested in doing a half hour programme with him. Of course, it was a very nice idea, but I had seen what the Germans were doing with colour television. It was in its infancy in those days and I noticed that whenever David did a show for them, they dressed the set with every conceivable brightly coloured object with a result that you could hardly see him. I thought no way were we going to have half an hour of this and thought why not make our own? I suggested it to Gunther and he agreed, wanting to have first viewing. We went home and made a half hour colour television film which was marvellous. It played a very, very important part in David's career because it was for that film that he wrote 'Space Oddity'. Most of the stuff on the film came from the Deram label but I thought we ought to have a very special piece of material — some new material — and something that would show how very fine and inventive a writer David was.

"So, off he went and came back one day saying that he thought he had the song I'd been looking for. He sat down and strummed it — it was 'Space Oddity'. It was obviously a very clever song but it wasn't until we were recording it and filming it down at Greenwich Studios, that we realized its potential because, during the break, after we'd done this segment of the film and had gone into the canteen for lunch, all the people who had been working on the film were whistling the song. As David walked into the canteen one of them said, 'Here comes Major Tom'. At that point we knew we probably had the makings of a hit.

"David had originally made a demo with John Hutchinson, a demo which had been taken to Philips who were releasing in this country for Mercury Records in America, and they all agreed that this would be the first single under that contract."

Mary Finnigan: "It emerged that David was

◀◀ *Lower Third Days.*

24

looking for somewhere to live. I had a spare bedroom and eventually, we agreed that he would come and live in my flat as a lodger — which is what happened. I thought I was getting David and maybe a few personal possessions, but when he actually turned up, he was with a friend in a very large van, and this rather ethereal, thin, slightly spotty figure that was David in those days, dressed in extremely scruffy clothes, emerged from this van carrying a 12 string guitar, which it transpired was a present from Pete Townshend. To my amazement, piece by piece, huge speakers, enormous amplifiers, old tape recorders and bits and pieces of audio equipment, along with mike stands and miles of wiring, was towed out of the back of this van.

"As I looked at this mounting pile of equipment I thought that there was no way this was going to fit into the spare bedroom. Of course, it never did. As soon as David moved into my flat, what used to be the dining room was no longer a dining room — it was now full of audio equipment, stylophones, keyboards, amplifiers and huge speakers. The whole flat, and the garden, within a very short space of time, was wired for sound and you would come in, perhaps in the middle of the night and fall flat on your face over wires and leads and God knows what. There would be blue sparks flying. It was really what one would describe as almost a complete takeover.

"After David had been there a couple of weeks, I used to go off doing odd bits of work in London working as a journalist, although I wasn't very keen on that side of my life at the time — there were other things that interested me more. It was a time when the whole underground culture was at its height and I was very much involved in that and had been since early '67. I was going through what could only be described a 'drop-out' period.

"There were quite a lot of drugs around at the time and somehow or other, I didn't quite know how, I managed to scrape enough together to feed my children and keep my flat going and just keep my life ticking over. Being a divorced lady and living on your own with two children, poverty can be a real problem when you lead that sort of life style. It was also a problem for David as well because he wasn't getting any gigs and he wasn't doing any recording work.

Mary Finnigan. ▶

"One evening, David, Barry, Christina and John Hutchinson were all sitting in my front room and talking about what we could actually do to earn some money. It was suggested that we might go down to one of the local pubs which held regular jazz nights, to see if they had an evening free and perhaps we could run a folk club just one evening a week and maybe charge people to come in and make a few pennies for ourselves.

"Having agreed that this was a good idea, David and I went down to a pub called the Three Tuns which is in Beckenham High Street. The landlord said that we could have the hall on Sunday evenings to run the club, and we could have it for nothing as he would make his money on increased bar sales. Events having turned out better than we expected, we returned to make our plans for the following Sunday when we intended to open. David designed the first poster for our first Sunday evening and stuck it up outside the pub. I had a friend who had one of those ancient slide machines which was used to give light shows, and you would make the slides out of coloured oils and inks and put them together between two sheets of glass and when they're heated up inside the machine, they went splat, splat and made these rather beautiful moving colours. The only problem was that by the time you had finished the slide show at the end of the evening you were covered from fingertips to armpits in coloured ink and oil and all the gunge associated with it. It may have been revolting but the effect was wonderful. But anyway we had this one projector which I had winkled out of this friend of mine, and we stuck it up on a couple of stools and hung some sheets up behind the corner of the room which served as a stage, and with some incense burning in the corner, an atmosphere was created.

"The idea was that David would be the anchor man, the resident musician, and every week we would have one paid performer who would be highlighted as the performer of the week, a tradition that was kept up throughout the history of the folk club and the Arts Lab. On the opening night, David did the major part of the entertainment himself, singing and playing tapes when he wasn't performing live. We used his P.A. system which was a bit ramshackle, but it worked — that was the main thing — and about 25 people turned up in the little mock Tudor, oak panelled dining room that was part of the Three Tuns pub in Beckenham. But it was a start.

"By the second week, it looked as if it was going to catch on. George Underwood designed the poster and 50 people turned up. We had doubled our audience. It appeared that we had fulfilled a need amongst people. We just hit at the right moment and from that week onwards, at least 90 people turned up every week. In fact, we were beginning to pack the place to the point where the landlord was extremely worried because there were far more people in than should have been. The club, by now, had spilled out into a sort of annexe conservatory at the back of the room and by the time the summer arrived, people were spilling out into the garden and, in fact, used to come into the club by this route illegally.

"It wasn't long before we discovered that there were many other talents around who wanted to be part of it. It was becoming something more than just a folk club. People came to read their poetry, they distributed their artwork, they hung paintings and pictures on the wall, and they came along with things they made like jewellery and candles and posters, selling them in the conservatory. All sorts

26

of little sub-businesses grew after the first month or two and it was at this point that we thought it would be nice to turn it into something more than just a folk club. So, one night, it was decided to ask the audience if they wanted an Arts Lab, and during one of his talks to the audience, as David also acted as compère, he asked whether they would like an Arts Lab in Beckenham, with the folk club being the start of it. The response was tremendous; the reaction incredibly enthusiastic, and so from that point, it became a little more than a folk club. It became the local community creative scene encompassing not only music, but mime, drama, poetry reading, and in fact, an outlet for local cottage industry. And that's how it all happened.

"All sorts of people since then have speculated on how the Arts Lab started, and various different books and publications about Bowie's career have put it in all sorts of different context, but that is how it happened. It was a thing that was created by popular demand. People wanted it and it seemed to be the right thing to do — so we did it.

"I remember on that opening night, a group of musicians arrived led by Roger Wootton, calling themselves Comus. They were to become, more or less, the Arts Lab resident band."

Roger Wootton: "David Bowie was the resident singer/song writer — a sort of folk-pop singer/song writer and we were a sort of rock/acoustic band — flute, violin, acoustic guitars and female vocalist, doing sets each week at the club which was the start of our career. David Bowie used to play material like 'Space Oddity', 'Janine', 'Port Of Amsterdam' — in fact the early material which appears on the 'Space Oddity' album which, at the time, hadn't been recorded. He used to just sit there with a 12-string guitar and often used a tape recorder with backing tracks, and then put on a harmony live or played a stylophone.

"He was rather fey, quiet, intelligent, but not particularly giving of himself. Hard to get to know in fact. To me, he seemed like an average folk-pop singer/songwriter. No more, no less. He wasn't particularly impressive live and in fact, the audience weren't particularly impressed with him. The only reason he was there every week was because it was his gig and he had arranged the Beckenham Arts Lab. He was sort of evasive and fey and appeared relatively shy and my impression of him at the time was that he had little charisma, no star quality and not a lot of talent, and it came as a big surprise when he became as successful as he was.

"The club itself was mainly hippies — art students and hippies — there were lots of drugs around and the Three Tuns used to stink of dope every week. There were lots of dealers there and lots of dope going around and David, to some extent anyway, seemed slightly an outsider, being very quiet and just arranging the gigs, but he was never really a part of what was going on. He didn't seem to be one of the other people. When I first met him he was just an averagely quiet spoken, fairly intelligent hippie and gradually, the perversity and debauchery crept in. He started wearing women's clothes, he started putting on make-up and on the last couple of times I saw him, he was pretty strange. By this time Angie had entered his life and she was going off with the ladies and he was going off with the boys — and that's the way it was."

Mary Finnigan: "Angie was very young and very wild in those days — real madcap. I got the impression very quickly that she was going through a

A Space Oddity – 1969.
▼

period where she was experimenting a lot with what she could get away with as an individual. She used to engineer situations by throwing freak-outs and being very off-the-wall on more than one occasion. It was a time before I began to understand her a little better and realize that a lot of this was actually a sort of 'attention-getting' — a bit of theatre just to see how people would react — to manipulate situations a little. It wasn't that serious. She was very young, 18 or 19, and relatively immature although much more worldly wise than I was because she had lived a much more international sort of life, and having been around the music scene a lot more than I had, she was streetwise at her age to a greater degree than I — there was no question of that.

"It was quite interesting how she first materialized. I had been away for the week-end and David Bowie is not the most domesticated person in the world. In fact, I would go as far as to say he's a slob. He always expected other people to clean up after him. He was totally oblivious of mess and basically needed an army of servants keeping things organized around him. If I had gone away for a couple of days, I returned expecting almost to have to push the front door open but to my amazement, the place was immaculate. I walked through one room after another. There was no dust, no dirt, no dirty dishes — it was tidy, neat as a pin, clean, sparkling and looked like it hadn't been touched, and I couldn't believe it. So, being a nosey bugger, which I am, I went into David's room and looked around for some evidence of what actually might have happened that weekend because I was completely stunned. Eventually, I found a song on a

scrap of paper by his bed. It was a song or a poem — I don't know which but to my knowledge, it has never been published — which was called 'Beautiful Angie', and I clicked immediately and realized there had been another woman about the house. Gradually, it became apparent that this lady was definitely part of David's life.

"Now my relationship with David did actually include sex, but it was never initiated on that basis as he'd come to my flat only as a lodger and during the course of the time he was there, we slept together. At the time, the idea of a strong, exclusive relationship was something that I did not actually want and I don't think that even consciously at that time, I would have sought to have had that kind of relationship with David who was considerably younger than me and also, even though I was deeply into the whole scene and everything it represented, I don't think I actually wanted to settle down with somebody who was a musician and was leading that sort of life style. But even so, when Angie first materialized I suppose I was a bit put out for two or three days. I was quite open to her presence and accepted her as part of the household and she charmed me very nicely — she was good at that. She was a very nice person; I liked her very much. She made a very positive effort to be the right sort of person to be around — in other words, she was not a liability, she was an asset, an extremely good cook and a very good organizer, and having discovered that we both went to the same school in Switzerland where French was the main language taught, we would enjoy talking to each other in French, much to the annoyance of David who couldn't understand the language."

Angie Bowie: "Mary and I got on really well — we had a hoot and always enjoyed each other's company, and although the Arts Lab was still running, it was beginning to get out of hand. It was changing into an enormous project with tentacle like bureaucratic things. It was now called Growth and to get a decision on anything, you had to have a committee meeting, and as I pointed out, if it was going to continue this way, David would lose interest totally. I could feel that the problem with David was very much a tremendous lack of application. A tremendous talent, but unless things were made very easy for him to get on and do things that he wanted to do, he would lose interest very quickly. Mary was aware of this too and tried very hard to explain to all of those other people who were involved. There were so many people that had become involved in this now enormous creature that resided in Beckenham called Growth. It got to the point where you would have one musical act and then you'd have to have a theatrical act, then you'd have a puppeteering act, all on a Sunday night under the guise of the Beckenham folk club.

"It was the psychedelic 60s and drugs were beginning to play their part in the Arts Lab, and I recall at one point David lecturing the audience on the dangers of taking drugs."

Mary Finnigan: "We were extremely righteous about our drugs in those days. Alcohol was considered bad news. Few people drank amongst our circle of friends. We smoked dope and people who wanted to would take sillacybin, mescalin or LSD, and that was literally it. There was nothing else considered to be OK. They were the drugs of awareness. They were not anaesthetics. They were things that you took to blot out life. They were things that you took to enhance your experience and to make it more intense — to make your personal development become part of your life. It was a very high-minded approach and when one looks at what has happened to the drug scene today and one looks back to the prevailing attitudes at the time, one can see the absolute, total abhorrence amongst drug takers that I knew in those days of amphetamines, heroin, barbiturates, mandrax — all those things that had an adverse physical effect which were considered to be highly dangerous to one's personal

development and to one's daily living.

"David used to get drunk and on many occasions I had to pick him up and carry him home from London, absolutely pissed out of his brain. He drank barley wine which is quite strong stuff and he'd smoke a few joints as well, but to the best of my knowledge, he wouldn't touch any hard drugs at all. During the time I knew him, he never took acid as he was very much afraid of it, and counselled other people against it in the sense that he felt it might disturb them psychologically, and felt that's what might happen to him. He didn't want to exacerbate what he saw as an existing weakness of his own in that respect, and although he was not censorious of other people, I think he was genuinely quite frightened of it, and at one point in the Arts Lab, when there was quite a lot of speed pills, amphetamines, going around amongst the young people there, he did speak out very strongly one evening against it, saying that he personally didn't want anything like that around anything he was closely involved with because he felt that it was not a good thing for people to be speeding and it created the sort of vibes that might end up causing problems. He was absolutely right in that respect and I remember him delivering this homily at the Three Tuns and the people receiving it in a rather stony silence because they were not used to being

◄ *The Three Tuns pub in Beckenham High Street. The home of the Arts Lab which was later to be re-named 'Growth'.*

Angie and puppeteer Brian Moore, an Arts Lab regular, with some of his creations (Bowie is under the table!) ▼

lectured. In fact, I think quite a lot of them took it to heart. He did see himself very much as a responsible figure as far as other people's well being was concerned when it came to this, and this was probably based on the fact that his step-brother, Terry, by his mother's previous marriage, was classified as schizophrenic, a problem which David felt could be hereditary."

Angie Bowie: "With the Arts Lab in full swing, Ken Pitt was ironing out the finer points of a new record deal with Mercury Records and in his own way was very lucid about David because he never actually saw him rooted in England or rooted only in rock and roll. He had arranged for him to fly to an Italian song festival which wasn't just Italian, it was an international song festival, of the lesser variety, but one which paid money. The first half was in Malta and the second half in Monsummano-Terme and arrangements had been made for David to fly out there with Ken Pitt and perform 'When I Live My Dream', one of the songs on David's first album. The plan was that I was to remain in England and organize the Arts Lab with Mary Finnigan and see it didn't fall apart."

Mary Finnigan: "It was at this time, when David flew out to Malta, then not only were we organizing the Arts Lab but a free open air festival in Beckenham. David, having flown out to the Maltese song festival had sent Angie a postcard saying something to the effect that he was going to be in Italy and why didn't Angie come and join him, which she did, leaving me to sort out both the folk club and the free festival organized for Beckenham Park the following Sunday."

Angie Bowie: "Anyway, I went out there and it was very romantic. It was not as I had expected at all because living in the kind of commune that Mary Finnigan's house was, there wasn't a lot of time for romance. It was a lot of sort of hippies pulling together to pull something off — hardly your Daily Mirror love nest, if you get my drift. Being quite intuitive, I did notice there was a funny tension between Ken Pitt and David and I thought that probably what had happened was that David had not been satisfied performing 'When I Live My Dream' with the old backing tracks, as he had been working with Tony Visconti and had all these new tunes and productions and ways of doing things in his head. I don't actually know — I'm surmising — but one tends to be fairly observant and that is what I felt.

"There had obviously been a couple of heated arguments, probably to do with artistic . . . you know, you get bored with something that you've done before and you're working on a new project, and I think he thought that having to wear a suit as opposed to his choice of stage gear can be very nerve racking. The suit he wore was fabulous — a sort of electric blue braiding, a nice little cabaret job. I don't mean to sound unkind, because it isn't. He looked very nice in it and he did win the contest, so Ken did know what he was doing. The problem was that I think David was moving so much away and into this trip of actually doing music with a message — of actually delivering something on stage which meant something to other people of his age. By now he had become aware that he had powers to lead people because of the Beckenham Arts Lab and Growth. He realized that he was somebody who could control people. If he actually put his foot down and said, 'No, I think that's ridiculous', everyone shut up and listened, and I feel that this

Angie Bowie pictured by Ray Stevenson. ▶

was the first time that he realised that he did have powers of leadership, not only on stage but also off stage."

Mary Finnigan: "While David and Angie were away with Ken Pitt at the song contest I received a telephone call from David's father asking when David would be back. I said I didn't know and thought no more of it and it wasn't until David returned and was performing at the Arts Lab on the Sunday night that I remembered and said to David, 'Oh, by the way, while you were away I had a message — your father is not very well'. He went ashen and screamed at me, 'Why didn't you tell me earlier?' He finished his set and was gone."

Mrs Margaret Jones: "David arrived home carrying the statuette that he had won at the song contest that he'd been to with Ken Pitt and dashed straight up to see his father who hadn't been well for a number of days. David handed the statuette to his father telling him that he'd won the contest and his father told him that he knew he would succeed in the end. He died not long afterwards."

Angie Bowie: "I was still in Cyprus when David called me. It was the most horrific thing. His father had died of pneumonia. My dad said he'd buy me a ticket to fly back to England and David said that he'd pay him back because he'd be very happy if I could come back and help him as he didn't really know how to deal with his mother's grief.

"I arrived to a house stricken with grief in Plaistow Grove, Bromley, and it wasn't easy. There were only two bedrooms and I had to share a bedroom with David's mother, a living arrangement that I just wasn't used to. I felt David's mother didn't really like me, and having to share a bed with her really drove me nuts. I tried to be as patient as I could and I think David's mother has realised for quite a long time that I was quite a good daughter-in-law to her (although I wasn't a daughter-in-law at that time) but as a girlfriend, I could understand her finding it obnoxious that her son brought some strange person into the house.

"She wasn't mean about it, she was very grateful to have someone to talk to and I used to try and spend a lot of time with her just to cheer her up — you know, walk the dog with her and go shopping — just do all the things that would help. But it was very trying and I don't know if it was like a part of me that was being grabbing or trying to weasel my way into David's affections. I don't think so because I'm not really like that and people who know me know that I'm not like that. I think I just put up with it because he behaved in such extraordinary ways to me in the time I had known him, of showing affection at all? Which he didn't show anyone else, and I felt privileged. I really thought I was probably not only his girlfriend but someone that he really trusted because he knew I was energetic and dynamic and could get things done."

Tony Visconti: "I remember when David's father died he was very solemn, as anybody would be when their father dies, and he took the responsibility of looking after his mother very seriously. I think his mother was a very low-key housewife who depended very heavily on her husband to do everything — to write the bills and all that — a very dependent housewife, and David automatically assumed the role of his father in matters of domestic finance. He appeared to grow up instantly and became very serious. I think his father's death had a very profound effect on him because his Dad was the only one who was level headed. Even David could be flippant and bizarre and go off and do his own thing, and Dad was the one person in the family who

◀

Mrs Jones, David's mother.

was the anchor."

Mary Finnigan: "A few days after the death of David's father, the free festival went ahead as planned and the day was fabulous; the sun shone and everybody but everybody had a wonderful time. There was music, puppet shows, street theatre, side shows, stalls. Angie was running the hamburger stall — I don't think she's ever cooked so many hamburgers in her life. The day was fabulous and David performed extremely well although he was in the blackest of black moods. He was extremely rude to a lot of people, some of whom vowed they would never speak to him again. Calvin Mark Lee, from his new record company, donated posters for us to sell at the festival and he was extremely rude to Calvin, which is very strange when you think of the lyrics to 'Memory Of A Free Festival' which he wrote after the event: 'I kissed a lot of people that day'. He certainly captured the feeling of that gorgeous sunny day in Beckenham Park, but it was not his own feeling. I think that he'd reached a stage in his life where he was to become less community minded and more geared toward the fulfilment of his own career."

Tony Visconti: "'Space Oddity' had been recorded and released at this time although it was not selling. In fact, I remember first hearing the song. We were putting an album together based on his light rock/folk style that he was developing — songs like 'Janine', 'Unwashed And Slightly Dazed' — all that country rock flavour that he was developing and then, out of the blue, he wrote 'Space Oddity'. Now I know David — he is very original. All his chord changes are very original and his melodies are. And here came 'Space Oddity' which was coinciding with men landing on the moon, which is what I think inspired him to write it, there is no question about it. David had come up with something that was extremely unoriginal. What I'm saying is, 'Here am I sitting in a tin can' sounded exactly like a Simon and Garfunkel record, and the rest of the song was lifts from everything else. Nowadays, I would probably have a complete reverse opinion and say, 'Well done David', but in those days I honestly didn't care. I wasn't going for his agreement or anyone else's agreement — I was going for what I felt was right at the time, and as he'd set me up as this person in his life, I advised him not to do it. However, everyone else advised him to do it and it was probably the most catalystic thing he could have done at that period, although I had the feeling even if he did get a hit, it was something he couldn't follow up because I knew the style of his writing. He wasn't writing anything remotely like it and he didn't afterwards. He just continued writing more of the same stuff that was going on his album. 'Space Oddity' was just one-off and it wasn't until 'Ziggy Stardust' that he did anything even remotely like it. Having told me that everyone was advising him to record it, I told him to go ahead and do it, but not with me. Gus Dudgeon, who I used on some earlier Deram sessions, said he'd like to work with David, so here was his chance and I put the two of them together."

Gus Dudgeon: "I was sitting back in my office and the internal 'phone rang and it was Tony Visconti, whose office was literally just down the hall. 'I've got an old pal of yours in here — David Bowie', he said. 'We're talking about making an album but he's got this song which I don't like at all, but you might care for it. Do you want to have a quick listen?' 'Sure,' I said. So, he popped down to my office, stuck this demo on the turntable and it just blew my socks off. I couldn't believe it. I rang Tony and said,

'You really can't be serious about not wanting to record this song.' 'I just don't like it,' he replied. I think he had a thing about it particularly because he knew the record company really was going for that song because the first American space shot was coming up. But actually, I don't think the record company realized just how good the song was. It was just that their minds went — 'Space Oddity' — guys are going into space — sounds like a commercial idea — go for it. So, the underlying part of the contract, as I understand it, with Bowie, was that he was going to make an album with Tony Visconti and that song had to be done as a single. But, of course, Tony didn't like the song, so he asked whether I'd do it, and that's how I came to do the record.

"I can remember the session very well. The players were Tony Cox on drums, Rick Wakeman on mellotron and Herbie Flowers on bass, who I learned recently, was paid £7.10 for that session, which was his first professional session. I recall I think we possibly planned to use strings right from the word go and David, without my knowledge, went to Paul Buckmaster and asked whether he was interested in writing the string parts. When Paul called me back to ask whether he was serious about this, I replied 'yes', although I must admit I didn't hear strings and flutes on 'Space Oddity' at the beginning but once the track was done, it was obvious that it was going to work really well. The other thing that I remember was that this session was very quick. As we were mixing the B side, this guy called Calvin Mark Lee, who worked for the record company, was actually off at Philips cutting the A side. Literally as we were mixing the B side he was over here cutting the A side. It was really high-pressure sort of stuff followed by this terrible waiting period, because no sooner did the record come out, and the space shot take off, the BBC banned every record that had anything mentioning the moon. They even banned an instrumental called 'Footsteps on the Moon' by Johnnie Harris. I think they were so nervous to play anything that would imply for the space shot or against the space shot — whether the guys were going to come back or not. It was pathetic really. So, no sooner did the record go into the charts and we were going 'yeah, this is it — hooray — we're taking off', they dropped the record and we had to wait for the guys to come back to earth. Luckily they came back without any harm and the record was then re-released, re-promoted and interestingly enough, as far as I can recall, it's one of the very early stereo singles. I seem to remember they put it in mono and did a limited edition in stereo which, for those days, was a fairly advanced piece of thinking.

"As a producer, 'Space Oddity' was very important to me as it was only my second or third hit record, and I was looking forward to seeing David play it live. The gig was at the Purcell Rooms and he was playing with a band called Junior's Eyes. Obviously, he built up to 'Space Oddity' being somewhere in the middle of the set and about half way through the set, he dismissed the band. I thought he was just going to do a couple of acoustic numbers. He went on and played 'Space Oddity'. Just an acoustic guitar and a backdrop of a sun shining. I couldn't believe it — what a weird thing to do. Like, here was his first big song and everybody had come to see it, and he's not going to do it with a rhythm section — just acoustic guitar. The whole audience was astounded and it didn't go down very well. It would have been far better if he'd done it the other way round — the rest of the set acoustic and then brought them on to play. It was just so bizarre.

Top inset: Ziggy beams down to earth. ▶▶

Haddon Hall, rare shot of the house where David wrote "The Man Who Sold The World", "Ziggy Stardust" and "Hunky Dory". ▶▶

Bottom inset: David performing on his first American visit, late January 1971. ▶▶

"Another amusing incident to come out of 'Space Oddity' was when I got a 'phone call from David one day, who said he had to record an Italian version of 'Space Oddity' because two kids in Italy had apparently done a cover version of it and as it looked as if it was going to do quite well, the Italian record company wanted a version by the original artist and said they would send somebody along to teach Bowie phonetically how to sing the song. Anyway, we went down to Morgan Studios in Willesden High Road and this Italian guy showed up at the studio. He was basically directing the session because I didn't know Italian, nor did David. He wrote out all the lyrics phonetically, so when he had to sing an Italian word, it was written down exactly how it should be pronounced. It was an hilarious session. At the end of it when the whole vocal had been recorded, David said to this guy, 'Just out of interest, is this my original lyric?' The guy said 'Oh no, it's a beautiful ballad about a boy and girl and they go out in the mist on the mountain'. 'Good God,' we said, 'are you serious? This is about people in space.' 'No,' he said. 'It's about a love story'."

Tony Visconti: "I heard the finished version of 'Space Oddity' that David had recorded with Gus Dudgeon a few days later and it was great. I figured that if this is what David wants and I'm not going to give it to him, then I'm perfectly happy to let Gus take over the responsibility since he did such a great job. But David surprised me by saying, 'OK, now we've got that out of the way, let's go and do the rest of the album'. He didn't believe in it himself. He said that he did it because everybody wanted him to do it, and he even agreed with me that bits were like Simon and Garfunkel and it sounded like a hundred songs written before, and admitted that he was cashing in on the moon landing but thought he could make some money doing it. Looking back, I said it would hurt his career. It didn't hurt it, but it didn't exactly help it. It was about two and a half years before he wrote anything like it again. But anyway, we finished the 'Space Oddity' album and promoted it a bit. I do remember we did a few gigs. I was on bass, David was on acoustic guitar and we got this guy called Tex, he was a black conga player and came around with us doing a few gigs, although nothing really happened. I remember we did a live version of 'Space Oddity' with acoustic guitar, bass and congas and it didn't go down so well."

Angie Bowie: "During this period we were still living with David's mother which certainly moved my rear end out into finding somewhere to live because having to sleep with someone really freaked me out. So I was looking around the Beckenham and Bromley area when I found this place called Haddon Hall which was an amazing property. It was the three main reception rooms of an old Victorian folly built for the Crystal Palace Exhibition, backing on to Beckenham golf course which, I suppose, became a very desirable place to be out of London in Victorian times. They built these houses onto the back of the park which became the golf course.

"It was an enormous red folly with balconies all around the back and to the gardens at the sides, and had been divided into apartments. There were seven flats in the building but the three main reception rooms and the hallway and the gallery which went round and then, of course, up to the upstairs room, had been blocked off. The hall and the gallery and the enormous stained glass windows which faced the door as you came in, and the three reception rooms were ours, and as I suffer from terrible claustrophobia, I thought it was a wonderful place to live although David, who I am sure doesn't suffer

Tony Visconti, David's friend and producer. ▶

from claustrophobia as badly as I do, being British and like most British people, would be content to live in smaller environments. He thought it was fabulous because I guess he just wasn't used to living in all that space and the idea of living in this enormous rambling series of rooms appealed to him very much.

"Unfortunately, prior to our moving in, 27 cats had lived there with a professor of history and his wife who were a little eccentric. There were a lot of plants and the cats felt they were in a jungle of their own in the hall. You can imagine the smell! But at 20 years of age, I had no scruples about rubber gloves and bleach, and dealt with the problem straight away. It was rather grubby so we just painted it all white and, as I suspected, David's imagination, after it was painted, came into heavy

personal lives. It was a very bizarre one — always turbulent and very strange. My girlfriend and I were a conventional hand holding couple and David and Angela were going to gay clubs at midnight and bringing home people at four in the morning which made things very tense, I would say."

Angela Bowie: "As Christmas drew near, 'Space Oddity' became a hit single in England, going on to win an Ivor Novello Award. Strangely enough, Ken Pitt wouldn't let me go with him, or his mother for that matter, to receive the award. Ken wanted to take David to this thing on his own and David, being very, very cold — he hates demonstrations of emotion — and me being very Mediterranean, I told him that as far as I was concerned, I didn't give a fuck about his award or seeing him receive it, but I thought it was a bit much that his mother couldn't be

Over page, the mod at work on Clapham Common. ▶▶

POLYTECHNIC ENTERTAINMENTS COMMITTEE
PRESENT IN CONCERT
DAVID BOWIE
BRIDGET ST. JOHN
ALAN SKIDMORE QUINTET

Sat., March 7th
10/- on the door

7.30 p.m.
BAR

EXTENSION BUILDING, LITTLE TITCHFIELD STREET

play.

"It took 6 months for us to talk the owner into agreeing to let us rent the place. I think this was due to the fact that we didn't have 9-to-5 jobs and were entertainers and couldn't possibly manage the £7 a week rent. In the end I remember I said to him that I was just a spoilt Yank and my father sent me money so he needn't worry about a thing. Anyway, we moved in. It was the coldest time of the year and the first thing I insisted on was having a telephone. David didn't think it was a good idea but I said we couldn't keep going out and using the 'phone box down the road. 'I'm telling you,' he said, 'it's not a good idea'. Little did I know how right he was because the first thing that happened when David's mother had a bad day, she would call me everything under the sun. Basically that David had moved out of Plaistow Grove to leave her on her own to die, to live with the fancy whore from America, and yet on other days, of course, I was perfectly lovely and would come and shop with her and do everything. Being as it was David's mother, an older person, it never occurred to me to get mad or upset. I would get mad when I put the 'phone down and cry a lot, but certainly I wouldn't get mad with her."

Tony Visconti: "When David and Angela found the enormous Victorian house, Haddon Hall, in Beckenham, my girlfriend and I went along to see it and we loved it. It was the most incredible place we had ever seen. It was like a little mansion. We decided to share the place together and pool our resources. It was very strange. I thought we could get on with him but I think within a week of moving in there we became entangled in David and Angela's

there because it was a public occasion and it was a time when, without having to speak to her, he could be nice to her, as every mother loves to be there for that kind of thing. David wasn't very happy about me being so blunt, but I think in a way it made him realize that I was really straightforward and that I really did care.

In New York in 1971. ▼

◄◄
Previous page: David at work in Haddon Hall on the design for Ziggy Stardust's next image.

"It wasn't long after the conversation about the Ivor Novello Award that he became much more resolved that he didn't need Ken Pitt as a manager, so I said to him that the only thing he could do in that case was to get an attorney who would break the contract. He replied that he had tried to get an attorney to break the contract and that he had spoken to this lawyer and that lawyer. At the time I was involved in various things at Philips Records and I asked someone there if they knew of anyone who could get David out of his contract, and was told that he knew a man called *Tony DeFries* who was actually not allowed to practise at the bar — he was a consultant, a trouble-shooter, divorce cases. He suggested we go and talk to him, so I said to David, 'Well, here's the guy — I don't know what he's going to do, but let's go and see him'. Which we did. DeFries was interested. He wanted to look at the contract and check it out and really, with no trouble at all — I think he wrote a couple of letters and said that Pitt was not acting in the capacity as manager that David required and that was that."

Ken Pitt: "I think the great problem was David was always very insecure and because he wasn't achieving the renown he wanted, like most artistes, he began to worry, bearing in mind that David was now living at Haddon Hall with a few of his friends, all of whom were unaware of what was going on in the office and how we were planning David's career, what progress we were really making. I think they just sucked up to David and began to put the boot in really, quite unnecessarily, and unfairly.

"As far as I understand it, it was Angela who pursued the interest in Tony DeFries. In fact, I didn't know until recent years that it was a person at Philips Records who in fact mentioned DeFries to David, and when he did meet DeFries, Angela was very much in favour of David moving from me to him. I think events proved that had she come to know me a little better, and talked to me, and tried to find out what I was planning and what I was doing, and how David's career was going, and co-operated with me to assist David, I think he would have had a much happier period ahead of him."

Angie Bowie: "I never realized and had never been involved in who did what, but I suppose that amounts to, if one wants to look at it from Ken's point of view, being the fly in the ointment, or if one was to look at it from a real point of view as, in terms of property settlement and management, that I was being David's manager at that particular time, because it was possible for me to advise him to do something about the things that troubled him artistically. I never really thought of it like that. I thought of it as just being a friend. I thought when someone gets miserable, you sort them out."

Ken Pitt: "However, I finished with him in April 1970. There was no animosity. It was a very friendly thing. We had a meeting in my flat. David said absolutely nothing — not a word. He said 'Hello' to me when he walked in and 'Thank you' when it was all over and he walked out. He just sat on the chaise-longue.

"Tony DeFries was rather diffident — a little restrained I thought. He wasn't the Tony DeFries that he became. We discussed the whole thing and I said there was absolutely no point at all. I think he was rather taken aback because my understanding is that he told David he could get him out of the contract. From this point David asked DeFries if he would become his manager. Well, of course, DeFries didn't get him out of the contract. He just came to me and said he was unhappy and I said OK. That's really all there was to it and Tony DeFries became his manager. David and I were very close friends and if he wasn't happy with what we were doing and wanted to change, I wasn't going to argue.

"A number of myths have grown up about David's relationship with me — one of them being that I wanted him to be another Tommy Steele or another cabaret star, but this was not true. At the time, David was going through what I suppose could be called an apprenticeship and he really didn't know what he wanted to do. We were trying to find out where his particular niches lay and the constant worry at that time was lack of money. His father would now and again telephone me saying that David was down to his last few pounds and that he worried about money. Not that it mattered very much, because he was living at my flat and wasn't going to starve, but I said to him, there is only one way you can make quick, ready money and that is going out on cabaret. I didn't recommend it to him because I'd seen what it had done to sensitive artists like Scott Walker. I said we could select the venues, he could write his own cabaret show; he could go out and do 20 minutes and pull £100 a week, which was a lot of money in the 1960s. I don't blame him — he didn't like the idea at all.

"So he continued trying to make a living the way he wanted to. Of course, he wasn't making a living at all and there was no way he possibly could. However, it got so bad one day — I think he had been discussing this with his father because he used to go home sometimes at the weekends and come back to the flat on Monday — and he came in one day and said, 'OK, it's going to be cabaret'. I thought that was a decision he and his father had come to over the weekend. I remember we set about putting together a cabaret show. It was a very progressive performance, far too uncommercial. However, it was a very good one. He wanted to do a Beatle medley and for that, we made four cut-out caricatures of The Beatles in hardboard and painted them and then fitted them on frames and easels so that they could be moved around and stood up. We decided eventually that the time had come to rehearse this seriously and he was very happy about it. We decided to show it to a booking agent who books cabaret, so I spoke to Harry Dawson who did a lot of cabaret work and we auditioned it for him. David was absolutely marvellous, a tremendous show, and when it was over, Dawson said to me, 'Ken, it's a marvellous act but it's too good — where can I book it?' Of course, he was absolutely right. It was the end of cabaret as far as we were concerned. The message got round and it got round Haddon Hall like wild fire that I wanted David Bowie to be a cabaret star. No way."

Tony Visconti: "The fact is that Bowie was becoming more and more disenchanted with Pitt. He was only getting him little gigs here and there and you wouldn't call him a dynamic person. David has always, for a time, hitched his rocket on somebody who is powerful — no question about it — he's powerful himself, but he needed an injection of ruthlessness which Ken Pitt, being a very sweet, nice man, wasn't giving him at the time. And then Tony DeFries just materialised. There's always a guy that says, 'I can get you out of this contract'. David was in a state at that time saying that he had signed these things years ago and wanted to get out. DeFries said he could get him out of anything. So that's how it happened, quite honestly. The way Tony DeFries went at it made me very suspicious. He said, 'What can I do for you?' and I said 'I didn't really want to get out of anything; I'm OK'. So his angle with me was that he'd get me work and get the money owed to me. He wrote a few letters on my behalf and I just didn't think he was for me because of what I saw at the time.

"So, David went with DeFries and I didn't. I wasn't by any means in love with the man. I thought he was all right, but I didn't think he was all that powerful, although I do believe in chemistry and obviously the chemistry between him and Bowie was magic — undeniably magic. At the time my feeling was that David was making a conscious decision to become big. He always did it for a while and then just let it ride to see what happened, but all of a sudden (it's amazing — I've seen it happen several times) he gets out of bed one morning and says, 'Right, I'm going to do something about it — it's not moving fast enough for me'. Usually, David at the time would surround himself with friends who did

Over page, David on tour in America and Japan in 1973. ►►

Kenneth Pitt, David's manager '66 to '70. ▼ ▼

Stage costume idea, later to be discarded. circa 1971. ▼

things for him, thinking that he would get things done out of loyalty. Then he would change people quite often when it didn't suit him to be with them any more."

Angie Bowie: "The Christmas before recording 'The Man Who Sold the World,' I had flown back home to see my parents. At the time there was a postal strike and I didn't hear from David for about 3 or 4 weeks. Then eventually, the strike was over, and the phone rang — it was David. He said that there had been a postal strike and that he had been trying to write to me and as the mail was getting through, I should get the letters. He wanted me to come back as, obviously, it was very helpful for him to have someone who would control things when he had to go out and work. When the mail did eventually arrive, I received this very strange Christmas card which said 'This year we will marry'. I nearly had a heart attack. With my father having agreed to give me £2,000, and adding, 'This is the third plane ticket I've bought for that man', I flew back to England and finished painting the house white, thanking God that I liked the art nouveau and Edwardian furniture that David had been buying, because otherwise it could have been tricky, having received that letter and realising that it might actually be love, it might actually be something serious going on.

"My father sent me the cheque, needless to say,

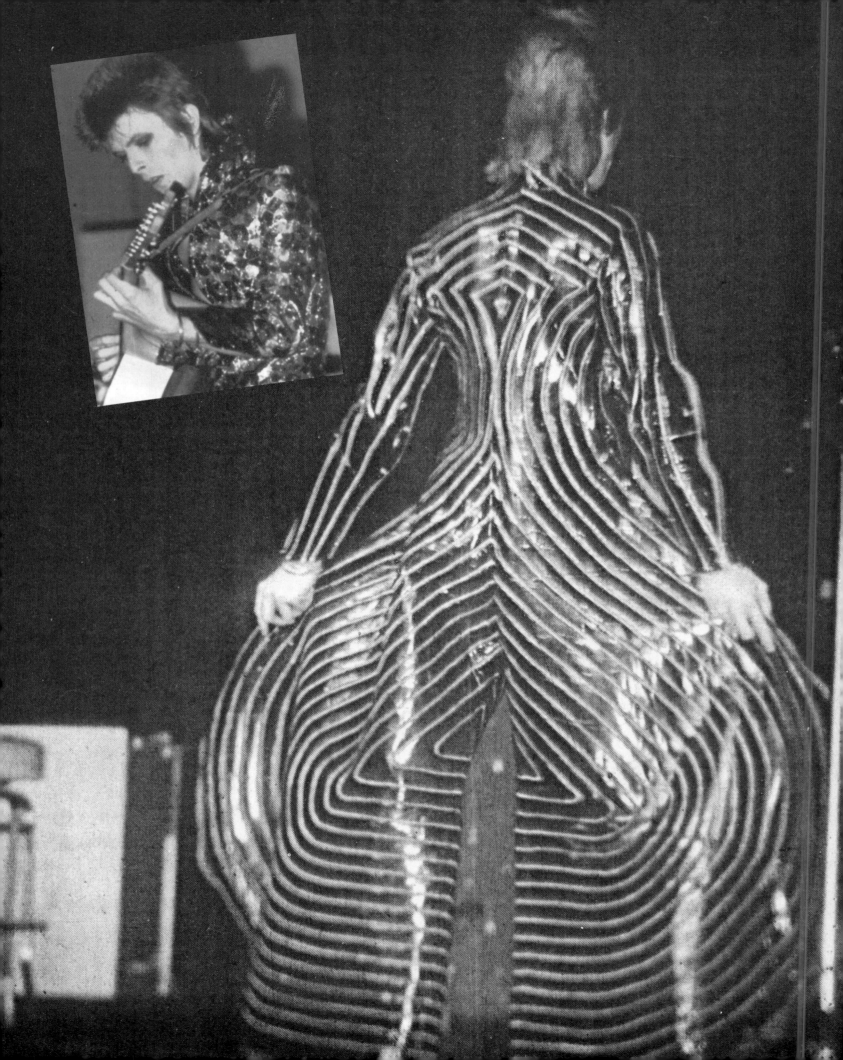

Wedding Day, 1970. David and Mary Angela Barnet. ▶

so David and I thought we'd better get married because that was the reason he sent the cheque. So, off we went to Kensington Market. It was so neat and we had a good time. David said, 'Let's go do it — let's get wedding duds', and I said, 'Absolutely'. So, off we went. Now it sounds like my father paid for it, but that's not true because David took care of all the stuff for the wedding. It was very cute. We got outrageous clothes — total outfits. David said, 'I hope nobody's going to be there', and I agreed, particularly the way we were going to look.

"On that evening, the day before the wedding, we went to visit our friend Clare Shenstone and her brother, friends of ours that we had met through Calvin Mark Lee. We went to her house and had dinner and stayed there all night. In the morning, we suddenly woke up and said, 'Oh, no — we're supposed to be getting married at 11 o'clock.' We raced down to Bromley and got to the registry office and there was David's Mum saying, *'You'll be late for your own wedding. There you are, I told you.'* I couldn't help laughing — it was so true. We were together. It's hardly as if one of us turned up and the other didn't. It was just one of those comedy of errors. 'It's all right. Don't worry,' she said, 'I've called the press.' 'What?' said David, dressed in black satin, looking absolutely outrageous, like a Lithuanian Dracula rock and roller about to get married and me in this sort of Victorian gown. It was too much. It was wonderful purple and pink, and very bright. All this and David's Mum having saved the day saying, 'Don't worry, I've called the press.' I

thought, 'Oh, no'. Needless to say, the press showed up. Little known rock and roller and American decide to get married. It was preserved for posterity with David's Mum smiling away — bless her heart. I don't know how David's Mum got there, because he decided not to tell her, even though I said he could call her because it's not really fair to get married without letting her know."

Tony Visconti: "At that time, we had gone into the studio to record 'The Man Who Sold The World,' and the horrible thing that was happening to me as a producer, the nightmare of my life, was that David and Angela were becoming totally entwined and enraptured with each other. If they were in a good mood, things would go well, but if they were in a bad mood, David wouldn't show up. Sometimes when they were in a needy mood, which was most of the time, David would be out in the lobby at Advision Studios where we were recording, and they would be cuddling and cooing and wooing — it was disgusting. I've got to tell you, it was disgusting. I suppose if you were either one of them it would be nice but I'd go out and say to them, 'David, it's time for us to do a vocal now' and Angie would say, 'Oh, Davey Wavey, do you have to leave me now?', to which he would reply 'Oh, Angie Pangie, I suppose I do — old Uncle Tony wants me in the studio'. It was absolutely nauseating to be involved with.

"The album didn't go smoothly at all. *Mick Ronson, Woody Woodmansey* and myself would be making up backing tracks, having got the brief from David — it was E chord for 16 bars then an A chord for 4 bars and a B chord for 2 bars — and we were just banging out these backing tracks, and David would come into the studio, if we could tear him away from Angela long enough and say whether he liked it or not. He wasn't asleep; it was just a very difficult time for him. He was juggling two different worlds. The musicians on one side and the great love of his life on the other and I could see his conflict, but it was my nightmare. It was my problem.

"We had about 6 or 7 weeks to finish the album and by the last week, I didn't have a vocal on two of the tracks and this is where it actually began — David writing on microphone. He'd start singing spontaneously. It was great. It was really wonderful. When he was hot, he was hot, but for me the whole thing was not so good. My two realities were getting this done technically to technical excellence, which I was struggling with as I didn't know my stuff so well then, and also, managing to get a good performance out of David. I had two big conflicts and would end the day a bag of nerves, not knowing whether I'd come home with anything. I had a record company screaming for final mixes, not even sure that they wanted this album because 'Space Oddity' didn't do too well and as far as they were concerned this was going to be the last they had to do with David Bowie, and I wasn't delivering the goods. A few

Rocking with Mick Ronson. ▲

thousand quid over budget. It was a nightmare, a really horrible period."

Angie Bowie: "By this time, David had left Ken Pitt and was with Tony DeFries. I think the death of David's father was probably what took him a while to make a decision about leaving Ken, because to lose his father, who he really adored, who had always been a pillar of strength to him, changed his life, and I think David carried a bitterness about him dying for a long time. I didn't want to get into soap opera conversation about it with him, but on the occasions that we did talk about it, both of us felt that someone, with perhaps a little more eye on reality, would have realized that he should have been in hospital and not at home and unable to reach the oxygen. For him to die of pneumonia was really a terrible waste and I think David harboured a little . . . you can't blame someone for something like a person dying tragically with pneumonia, but I think he felt that maybe his mother should have watched over him more carefully, but I suppose that's like saying the cat got drowned, why was there a puddle there? It's a stupid thing, I used to try really hard not to get involved in those conversations. His father was a public relations man for Dr Barnardo's Homes and could chat away and do all that kind of thing, whereas David was very much like his mother in terms of showing affection.

"It was like every time I got a letter or an insinuation from him that he cared, or that he really loved me or wanted me to be with him, it shocked me because he wasn't good at showing that. It was for this reason that I had Zowie because I could see how he was with children. Children really drew him out. He could get involved with children and be affectionate and spend time with them. I get very bored with reading how difficult he is and how cold he is. He's not like that. He's a fabulous guy and very funny, but it took a long time, and I don't take credit for it, but it took a long time to put him in a situation where I felt that he was at maximum 'comfortableness', so that his shyness — and he was very shy — was overcome.

"It was like all that ego-building which eventually turns into a monster. It was very necessary because he was so unsure. Not of his talent — he always

◄

The first of many. David interviewed in New York for his first promotional visit of 1971.

►►

Over page, travelling 'Soft' on the Trans Siberian Express, David still in his dressing gown.

Photo: Leee Black Childers.

43

David jams with Marc Bolan on his last TV show. ▶

knew he was good and he always knew what a great songwriter and performer he was — but for instance, he was nervous of audiences. The idea of touching people in the crowd or letting people in the crowd touch him was something that had not occurred to him, but to be that beautiful and that remote . . . you've got to get a crowd to touch him because that was what really got them wild. That was what caused the hysteria and the enthusiasm and so, I felt that if the band on stage was at least so close to his sense of humour that he felt comfortable with them, if the crew and all the support system was so strong that he could relax enough to enjoy the crowd, only then would it get magnetic and really spontaneous. He relied on me a great deal because he knew I always knew what to do. It was only when we were very close that he would say he was shy."

David had almost completed the album, 'The Man Who Sold the World', and it wasn't long afterwards that Tony Visconti moved out of Haddon Hall.

Tony Visconti: "When it was finished, on the last day of the last mix, I remember telling David, 'I've had it. I can't work like this any more — I'm through. I've got Marc Bolan who wants to record day and night and is keen to go, and I might as well put my energies into him because you really don't want to work very hard'. David was very disappointed.

"I remember the final time I saw him. It was outside Tony DeFries's office on the corner of Regent Street and Great Castle Street. I just said 'Goodbye' to him right then and there. He looked at me very quizzically. He was in pain. 'But why?' he said. 'I told you, I can't deal with this any more,' I replied 'and I don't like Tony DeFries.' It's funny, I never really did like him and Ken Pitt thought I always wanted them to be together. It was clearly David's choice and that was it. That was the last time I saw David for about four years."

Posing with Freddi Burretti, aka Rudi Valentino of Arnold Corns (one of Bowie's experimental bands). ▶▶

In happier days. A rare shot of David with Tony DeFries and Angie Bowie, Chicago, October 1972. Photo: Mick Rock. ▶

THE AMERICAN DREAM

T H R E E

The Arts Lab faded into the distance, "Space Oddity" was a successful single but the album aroused little interest. David, having parted from Ken Pitt, was now managed by Tony DeFries. The follow-up album, "The Man Who Sold The World", which caused a parting of the ways between David and Tony Visconti, was also released. David called Mick Ronson and Woody Woodmansey (after making "The Man Who Sold The World", they had returned to Hull where they lived) and invited them back to prepare for the next album, "Hunky Dory". He informed them of Visconti's departure and the need for a replacement bass guitarist, and they returned with a friend who played bass called Trevor Bolder. Collectively, they moved into Haddon Hall with David and Angie. Meanwhile Tony DeFries was negotiating a new recording deal with RCA. Peter Noone, formerly Herman of Herman's Hermits, recorded "Oh You Pretty Things", a song written by David, which entered the British charts and oiled the gears of the DeFries negotiating machine.

On May 28, 1971, Angie gave birth to *Duncan Zowie Haywood Bowie,* an event that David documented by writing "Kooks" for the *"Hunky Dory"* LP.

In August *Andy Warhol's* production of *Pork* opened at The Roundhouse in London. The cast of this production would play a major role in the MainMan organization set up by Tony DeFries to handle David's career': *Cherry Vanilla* would become Press Agent, *Jamie Andrews* an Administrator, *Tony Zanetta* David's Personal Assistant, and *Leee Black Childers* the MainMan Staff Photographer.

Leee Childers: "The production was made from Andy Warhol's personal tapes. He used to tape everything — every conversation, every telephone call, everything — and we put it together into a play. We first performed it in New York where a crazy art dealer decided to bring it to London, so to London we came. None of us had ever been here before and we were all living together in one flat, which we called Pig Mansions, in Earls Court. Cherry Vanilla and I used to take care of our time when we weren't rehearsing by pretending we were rock and roll journalists — which we weren't. I pretended I was the photographer and she pretended she was the writer. We called up all the record companies to see shows and they let us go and see all the shows because we had American accents and we were crazy.

"Every week, we got the New Musical Express and looked to see who was playing, and one week I saw a little, tiny ad for David Bowie at a place called The Country Club on Haverstock Hill which, as it turned out, was like a garage behind a row of shops.

I'd read a little article by John Mendlesohn in *Rolling Stone,* which emanated from the trip he took to Los Angeles the year before, which must have been about 1970, that said that there was this guy who did weird songs and dressed up in dresses. We thought anyone who dresses up in dresses we want to go and see. So we called round but couldn't find a record company, although by this time he was with RCA. He was just doing the 'Hunky Dory' album but we didn't know that. Anyway, we got in touch with The Country Club and they put us on the guest list and Cherry Vanilla, Wayne County and I, posing as journalists, went along to see him.

"When we arrived, there were only about 20 people in the audience and he wasn't dressed in a dress. He was in yellow trousers and big hat. *Mick Ronson* was with him and Rick Wakeman on piano. Angie was there too, and *Dana Gillespie.* Angie was very loud at the time and being really crazy, so we all got on famously. We were a little disappointed — or at least I was — with David because he wasn't in a dress and he wasn't nearly as crazy as we thought he would be, but nevertheless, we liked his music a lot and he introduced us from the audience and Cherry Vanilla stood up and popped out a tit for the other 20 people, and David said that we were doing *Pork.*

"David and Angie came to the opening night of *Pork* and to nearly every night thereafter and we became really good friends. We went out with them to Yours And Mine and The Sombrero, and we danced and found them all very crazy. Then the show ended and we had to return to America and I thought that was that — good friends, really talented, I'd grown to really like David's music. It was at that time, in fact, that he met Andy Warhol. Actually I think it was at the opening of *Pork* because Andy came to the opening and David had that song on the 'Hunky Dory' album called 'Andy Warhol', so we made sure they met."

Dana Gillespie: "I'd just come back from the States and was hanging around with a band called Ashton Gardner and Dyke. In fact it was about that time that David and I both auditioned for *Hair,* and we were both turned down which I thought was quite funny because it seemed that just about everyone else in London got the part, but we were very much the kind of solo singers and perhaps the wrong type. Anyway, I was doing *Catch My Soul,* which was a rock Othello, starring Jack Good who was playing Othello himself, P.J. Proby and P.P. Arnold. David and Angela came along to see it and David said, 'I must introduce you to this guy Tony DeFries who is going to be my manager, and I think you should meet him too'. So, I went with him to meet DeFries.

"They were in offices in Regent Street with Lawrence Myers and a lot of song writers like Tony

◄◄
Previous page (right), main pic – David photographed at the Grammy awards of 1975 with John Lennon, Yoko Ono and Roberta Flack.

◄◄
Previous page (left), Diamond Dog and Soul tour shots from '74/'75.

McCauley and Mike Leanders pottering about. I walked in with David and there was this guy with a mass of curly hair sitting behind a desk, looking very Jewish — not like the Jewish businessman, though he is a wonderful businessman. We got on very well and from there came the start of MainMan. MainMan wasn't started right at that point but then DeFries had the idea that he could keep a better eye on David, myself and eventually Mick Ronson, as he was treated as a solo artist.

"One of Mick's first jobs concerning David was to organize the arrangements for my album which later became 'Weren't Born A Man'. We first did about five tracks which was pressed on a private white album, with me on one side and David on the other. I can't actually recall all the numbers, but I remember I was in the States at one point and I took this album over and tried to sell it to a record company. In fact, I went to a couple of record companies and said 'This is me and David Bowie'. They said 'Thanks, but no thanks'.

"Then came the period when I used to hang out a lot just with DeFries, and we'd drive down to David and Angie's place in Beckenham, Haddon Hall, on Sundays, and Angie would cook and we'd sit around. I remember David would always watch television if the The Alwin Nicholas Dance Company was performing, or there was a programme on Kobuki Theatre or something. He never watched boring Coronation Street type programmes.

"David had always been a great fashion person as well. He was the first guy I ever saw in military clothes before the main craze for the mods dressing up in military uniforms went on.

"I remember on one occasion the four of us went down to the Glastonbury Fair where he sang, but due to a balls-up over the sound and the electricity, they didn't put him on until the next day and that was at about 5.00 in the morning when the sun came through. He was standing on this big silver pyramid where the stage was. People had been very cold and

were sloshing about in the mud from the day before. They were in their plastic bags on the outdoor grounds, and as the sun came up, it came up over the top of the hill and hit the silver pyramid and there was David on stage singing. I think he was singing 'The Sun Machine Is Coming Down' or one of those. It was a great number and they took notice of him even though he was just on his own. His hands were so cold he could hardly play the guitar. I was standing on the side of the stage watching him. It wasn't long after that MainMan was completely formed."

Leee Childers: "After playing in *Pork*, I'd been back in America for about a year when the 'phone rang — it was Tony DeFries, David's manager, who I had apparently met before but didn't remember. He said that David was getting ready to tour America, but he didn't want normal rock and roll people — he wanted weird, crazy people to be his staff and he asked whether we'd do it. Would we become MainMan America? Cherry Vanilla was

doing nothing — she was eating fruit and breaking out all the time as a result, Jane was doing nothing too — she'd started a group called Queen Elizabeth which played little, low-life funky bars on the Lower Eastside, Tony Zanetta was working coding, which is a very ignominious job that out-of-work actors do in New York, and I was working at *16 Magazine* as a tea boy. None of us had anything to lose, so we said, 'Sure, of course we will'. Little did we know that it would result in one of the most amazing periods of any of our lives — including David's I'm sure. It was quite bizarre. So that's how I got involved.

"'Ziggy Stardust' had just been released in England and David was doing well with it, or so I'm told, but no-one had heard of him at all in America, so Tony DeFries gave us each a box of 25 albums to just give to whoever we thought was cool, which actually turned out to be a pretty good idea. We took them down to Max's Kansas City and gave one to Micky Ruskin the owner, we gave one to the DJ; and we gave one to Lisa Robinson, the reporter. We

◄◄
Leee Black Childers - Mainman 1.

◄
Cherry Vanilla - Mainman 2.

►►
Over page, the Thin White Duke, 1976.

51

just passed them out to crazy people and artists and people who were always on the scene in New York. Then Tony asked us to find him office facilities. Money, apparently, was no object, although there was no money. He kept saying, 'Money is no object — find me what I need'. And we kept saying, 'You have to pay for these things'. He'd say, 'Don't worry, don't worry about that. I'll deal with it. There'll be money. . . sometime'.

"All of us were working on no salary, just expenses, but we found nice facilities on 58th Street and were taught to charge everything. We got charge accounts at Max's Kansas City, we got a charge account with a limousine service — we rode limousines instead of taxis because we didn't have to pay for limousines and we'd have to pay the taxis — so we were always in limousines. We got charge accounts at Bloomingdales and stores like that, so we were always dressed fabulously and we were always sitting around in fabulous restaurants, charging for fabulous meals with all manner of people, which was all Tony's plan to make it look like the most successful rock and roll company going. And it worked."

Dana Gillespie: "DeFries always thought that in order for us to absorb musical culture as it should be from America, we should actually go and live in America, and it took quite a few months for it all to be organized. I was at that time in *Jesus Christ Superstar*. It was 1973 and already we were preparing for the move to the States. I'd started my album 'Weren't Born A Man' and Mjck Ronson was the arranger and producer for a couple of tracks, and David produced a couple of tracks too, but during the making of the album, David became even bigger and bigger in America and the move to America was absolutely imminent so I had to finish my own album without the help of him because he wasn't around — which I did.

"His interest in what was going on in America was always strong. I remember when the Andy Warhol lot came with *Pork* to The Roundhouse — we all went off specially to see them and meet them afterwards."

Leee Childers: "In America, we'd go to the record

Dana Gillespie. ▼

companies and make outrageous demands at RCA because we didn't know any better. We didn't know that we were asking for impossible things, because we had never worked in the record business before — and we'd get them. We'd get our demands because anything was done to shut us up and get us out of their offices. We just prowled around the halls at RCA at the time, going in any doors that were open and asking for things and demanding things.

"We'll never know whether it was Tony's plan or David's plan. We had this debate all the time amongst us — who was the actual person behind the grand design? Was it Tony DeFries or was it David Bowie? I guess we'll never know looking back on it, various things can be traced to David and other things traced to Tony. We think, but we don't really know what they were saying to each other behind closed doors. But anyway, we created that whole idea that no–one could photograph him, no–one could do a story on him unless it was going to be a cover story, which was outrageous because he was virtually unknown in America. To ask for things like that was totally beyond what an experienced person would ask for. An experienced publicist would go for a colour piece somewhere instead of the cover, but we were instructed to only go for cover pieces, so we ended up getting them of course, and we ended up creating this whole myth around him which was fabulous.

"I was the advance man. I was the person who was supposed to go to every city before David got there to make sure that everything was in order, that the hall that was going to be performed in had all the facilities that were required — and the hotels — I had to check all of that. I'd never done any of that before either. I was given a list of 12 absolutes that if the promoter could not provide, I was to cancel the gig on the spot.

"I remember the very first gig I went to in Cleveland, the grand piano was two feet too short. I was terrified, so I called New York. I told them that the grand piano was two feet too short and DeFries said, 'Cancel the gig — no gig'. Cleveland was the big David Bowie stronghold — he'd broken in Cleveland whereas he hadn't in New York and places like that. I said, 'The show's sold out — the place is really nice'. Tony said, 'Cancel the gig'. So, I cancelled the gig and they got the piano that was the right size and the gig was back on. That's the way it went for the whole tour. If one little thing wasn't on, the show was off.

"By the same token, Tony DeFries had a clause in the contract that if the promoter lost money he would pay it to him, so it was impossible for a promoter to actually risk anything. They would definitely, at least, break even, and it did come to bear a few times. In St. Louis, we were booked in an 11,000 seater hall and I think 180 or so people came. From a financial point of view it was a disaster and I saw Tony DeFries actually pay the difference to the promoter. That way, of course, the promoter would re–book. You don't lose. There's no risk. From an artistic point of view, it was one of the best shows and the kids were scattered about this huge place based upon what priced ticket they had bought. David was absolutely unbothered. He came out on stage and called them all down to the orchestra pit right in front of him. All 180 kids gathered right at his feet and he did a completely different show from any show that he'd done in the sell out places for five or six thousand. He did a really intimate show where he sat on the edge of the stage with his ankles crossed and talked to them and sang them songs. It was a whole different show.

"Occasionally, he'd bounce back on stage and do the whole thing with the strobe lights and everything which sent one poor little girl who had epilepsy into a fit. But apart from that incident, it was a great show and he did the same kind of thing in Seattle, Kansas City and the sort of cities in the Mid West where they hadn't heard of him — it was too early — but Tony DeFries was as good as his word. He always paid the promoters if they lost money.

"The tour was originally booked, I think, for about eight cities starting in Cleveland, then Memphis, then New York. He wanted to do a bit before New York and it worked because before the tour started, there was very little interest in New York, but it sold out in Cleveland which we knew it would, sold out in Memphis which we knew it would, and both shows were great, by which time word got back to New York instantly, as it does, and by the time the show at Carnegie Hall happpened, it was sold out.

"The audience was ready for a great star because they'd heard that he was. It worked beautifully it was a fabulous sensation. Then it was meant to be Detroit, Chicago, St. Louis and work its way west and end in Los Angeles but word of mouth, the cover story in *Rolling Stone* which Tony coerced out of them, and various other things created such a sensation that they lengthened it. That's why we went on to Seattle and Phoenix and worked our way back east again through the south, through Texas, Florida and Tennessee and it ended up going on more than twice its length because of the success of the show.

"I left before the tour was over because it was time for Mott The Hoople to come and tour and I'd been designated as the person to take care of them, so off I went before it was over. But he did do three fabulous nights in Philadelphia and Boston again. It went on and on and that was what solidified him in America. He still hadn't had any chart hits at the time and in fact didn't until 'Fame'.

"David had always liked Mott The Hoople and admired them, and I think it was one of the few really unselfish acts he did when, when they were on the verge of breaking up, he wrote them a song — 'All The Young Dudes'. As far as I could ever determine, he really did do that — he actually sat down and wrote a song for them because he liked them and didn't want them to go away. Having written the song, he gave it to them. He was not a big star at the time and it was just a good song. He wasn't trading on his name; he didn't think that that would have any particular influence. He wrote it purely because it was a song that was right for them. And it was. Having given them the song, it was a hit and that's when Tony DeFries picked up the management. They were a difficult band to manage because they were always on the brink of breaking up. They were all very highly strung and eventually, they did break up. But David really liked them. He used to go to their shows and just show up out of nowhere."

Angie Bowie: "Prior to the American tour, the 'Ziggy Stardust' album had been released and David had already completed a tour of England. I think it was a great relief for him to think that Tony DeFries would deal with things and all he had to do was deal with his artistry. I don't think he conceived 'Ziggy Stardust' as a concept album, but the songs slotted together in a way that it became a concept, and the way he presented it on stage, how he wanted to look, how the boys' costumes looked (facsimiles of his — though his were patterned and theirs were

simple) meant that he'd breathe life into a concept hero. I think he got confident. I think he got confident of knowing what he could do. I think Tony gave him confidence because Tony looked after the day–to–day worries of how one paid for what one was going to do.

"Going into the studio — you have a record deal that says the record company pays for that — but has that contract been examined? It took a lot of worry away from him. The band were very supportive and knew they didn't have to do anything untoward. They just had to be there and play well and perform well. And they enjoyed it. They loved the fact that Tony and everyone was dedicated to making it happen. It was an ideal situation for someone in that vernacular. I think that it was probably the moment that his insecurity was surmounted. He really became able to deal with whatever insecurities he had as an artiste or I hope that's what it was."

Mick Ronson: "It was a really exciting period then because Tony DeFries got involved, which was about maybe a year and a half after I first played with David. It seemed to be like, 'Don't worry about the money and if you need equipment you get the equipment, if you need clothes, get clothes made'. Everything seemed to be taken care of and everybody was on a real high because it left you free to do what you wanted to do without worrying about paying this week's rent or buying a pair of shoes, or whether a valve in the amplifier had gone and you had to replace it. All those sort of things. So all those things went out of the window which makes life much easier. It was really exciting just to carry on and get involved in making an album — get on the road.

"I think it started before 'Ziggy Stardust' — it started around the 'Hunky Dory' period with the clothes and I think we started off playing as a duo in the 'Hunky Dory' period. We'd get Rick Wakeman to play piano on a date and then we'd add someone just playing bongos. I think Woody played bongos on a couple of gigs or something, but it was a very acoustic thing and that's why 'Hunky Dory' sounded

►►
Over page, David and CoCo visit a Paris floor show.
'78 tour shot/ with Angie arriving for a TV show in LA.

Over page (right), David on the Rona Barret Show in 1976. ►►

Mick Ronson.
▼

like it did. But then it seemed to snowball from 'Hunky Dory' into 'Ziggy Stardust' because after playing one or two gigs as an acoustic outfit, it seemed to be natural to take it that step further — to add the bass and add the drums and make it bigger and better — more of a show of it — and so it evolved into 'Ziggy Stardust'. I think David had one or two of the songs off 'Ziggy Stardust' way before and so it became a natural progression to do that. It all seemed to snowball very quickly."

Angie Bowie: "I think basically 'Ziggy Stardust' was a good album and they played the parts really well. I insisted they look great all the time. I told them they couldn't expect people to get excited by four scruffy ragamuffins that came in the stage door and then go put on their party clothes, which were fantastic, and then again put on their horrible Levis and leave again. I said 'You're going to get mobbed coming in and you're going to get mobbed going out, so you'd better look good coming in and going out'. The street clothes had to look as good as the stage clothes. Added to which, David had been interviewed by *Melody Maker* and said he was gay which gained a lot of publicity."

Mick Ronson: "At the time when that story came out, my family in Hull took a lot of flak about it because they'd never even heard about it up there. It came like throwing paint over the car and paint up the front door and stuff like that, which really annoyed me. It's pretty sad. Some people thought I was gay. I wasn't gay and when somebody asked me I'd say, 'No, I'm not' which was the truth. That's what I had to say about it. If somebody doesn't like the truth then it's too bad. It was a bit of a pain for a couple of weeks. It was very short lived but at the time it was a bit of a shock. It wasn't a shock amongst ourselves — it was more of a shock from other people's reactions. For instance, throwing paint over the car and my mother going through it. People were really annoyed up North. That was something at the time that I felt I didn't really need myself.

"I think the other thing was that I wanted to be known as a musician rather than some other phenomenon other than a musician and I think that also had an effect on me too. Maybe people were seeing me as something other than what I wanted to be naturally.

"Audiences like to see a bit of theatrics here and there. They like to be able to go to a show and to be able to see something that they don't see in their everyday lives — you know, catching the bus to work or coming home on the bus. When people go out for a night they like to come away with being entertained. Or, if it's not being entertaining, coming away absolutely hating it or loving it — as long as it's some sort of reaction. I think people like that because people's lives are pretty dull on the whole.

"Angie was great because she was always very enthusiastic. Much more than I've ever seen anybody. With me coming from the north of England, everybody is pretty reserved up there at the best of times, so coming down to London and meeting Angie with an American accent and flitting around the room and speaking in a loud voice all the time, it was amazing. She actually did a lot of good things — she pulled a lot of things together and did a lot of things for David. Just her enthusiasm alone. If you had any doubts about doing anything, she would be the first to say, 'Don't be silly, you can do it'. It was very good to have somebody like that — someone who keeps pushing you and telling you that you can do it and not to be shy."

Angie Bowie: "That first American tour was interesting. The boys were good. The American audiences were kind of small at first and it was a major promotional coup to have survived it all because a lot of dates were pulled at the last minute — promoters couldn't get any interest. We'd go and be about to play a town and that town pulled out. Then we'd be sat for two or three days until another show was put in. But David was fabulous — he was just great – and the boys were great. Everything about it worked. The only thing that didn't work was the understanding that we had to be big time very quickly. The boys were big time, but we had to have the sound system, the lighting, the stage — everything had to move at the pace of David's imagination. The shows in New York were incredible. In fact, all the shows that played there were amazing although we did two or three shows in America where there weren't a lot of people. They had large capacity halls — maybe three or four thousand — and there were maybe two thousand people there, which was funny for the boys because they weren't used to that. They were already getting used to the fact that they were very popular. Even though they might be cult, they were very popular cult.

"That first tour did a lot to make the rest of the tours tremendously successful because, with all things like that, if you do play to a small group of people and you still do a great show, then by word of mouth the word spreads how wonderful you were, even though it wasn't packed. It stays with them — very omnipresent in their minds. They remember that and they love you for it even more, so when you go back, you have this staunch hard core group of fans that really bring things like that to a head, that really make it happen for you. They're the ones that call radio stations and demand more airtime, scream when the station is not playing the new album, and eventually cause it to happen for you."

Tony Zanetta: "Prior to his tour of the States, David started doing dates in England and within three months he was becoming what seemed like the biggest thing in England. Within another month or two, he did The Rainbow which got enormous coverage, and within another month he was here getting ready for the first American tour. It all happened really quickly. That first tour in America was not really a tour. It was random dates — it wasn't properly organised, it was just eight dates — and to bring thirty people over was kind of lunatic. But it worked. He came with his random dates and began touring. We all learned very quickly and we learned how to do it fairly quickly. Within a month or two, we were getting pretty good at it. There was a lot of waiting around — waiting for more dates. There was no money. That was the main thing, there was very little money, so we charged everything. DeFries had an idea that to be a star you should act like a star, so everything was first class. Everyone stayed at the Plaza Hotel. There were limousines and flowers and champagne. There was money for silly things. DeFries gave everyone money to get winter coats when he decided it gets cold in the United States. The money would pay for everything anybody needed, but no–one had more than five or ten dollars in their pockets. We were all forced to stay in hotels and eat in hotels and sign for it.

"RCA had agreed to certain kinds of support that got out of hand. They were willing to charge the hotels against royalties. The room service kind of crept in and since we didn't have any cash, we charged meals. We charged everything. We sat in the Beverley Hills hotel for two weeks and ran up

The smile of success '72 style.

Over page, David filming the May Day Parade in Moscow, 1973. Inset with Catherine Deneuve at Heaven night club in the film 'The Hunger'. ▶▶

about $20,000 worth of room service. People didn't have money for taxis so we took limousines. We could get a limousine at the Beverley Hills hotel but you couldn't get a taxi, so everyone learned how to call down from the front desk and order whatever they needed out of necessity. It created this mushroom kind of thing that people stared at. It was total insanity. It looked like there were just fortunes being spent, which there were, but no–one could quite figure out where the money was coming from, or why this money was being spent in this way. It was all a little 'circussy' — a little P.T. Barnham. I'm not saying it had such a positive effect on his career but it caused a lot of attention to be focused on him and he was able to live up to that attention, attention which he didn't buckle under, and I do feel a lot of people couldn't have lived through that experience, but he did. He got a lot of attention.

On the Trans Siberian Express '73. ▶

"By the end of that first tour, he was on the cover of *Rolling Stone*. He had started out in Cleveland, Ohio playing 3,000 people — he went back to Cleveland within two months and played to 20,000 people. In Philadelphia, it was like The Beatles had arrived. There were fans everywhere and people chasing after him in the streets. It was all very exciting and again, because none of us had gone through it before, it was really wonderful to watch this happen and to be part of it.

"It also began to get weird. Maybe not the first tour but by the second tour, I think it began to get decadent. But first it wasn't. It was very innocent and naïve, but it was corrupted. You know, staying at The Plaza and ordering champagne whenever you wanted — it does something to you. Also, you think you deserve it or you think you've earned it or you think you can afford it, and everyone began to act like that. The arrogance began to creep in. I think in a way we were all Ziggy Stardust and we were all living out this myth of Ziggy Stardust and treated him as if he was Ziggy Stardust. We began to treat him like a strange alien person who needed to be over-protected, who needed to be shielded from outsiders and the press. Then we would read about it in the press and it was all self perpetuating. An incredible arrogance and corruption and decadence set in. It didn't really happen overnight I guess, but through the MainMan News, MainMan kind of mushroomed into this enormous spending machine that really got out of control and I think was a very destructive influence on everyone that was involved."

Dana Gillespie: "In the high flourishing finance days of MainMan I had a secretary, a wonderful car, limousines everywhere, first class tickets everywhere and bills paid for everything at places like Bloomingdales. MainMan really looked after their artistes extremely well. I would be flying over and staying with Angie for a couple of weeks at The Sherry Netherland, and Angie and I would go with Zowie in the daytime and then we'd stay up all night with David because he functioned at night. Or Jagger would come over from the next hotel and we'd have late night 'looning' sessions, and then Angie and I would go off again with Zowie. We actually got really tired.

"In 1974 I was at the National Theatre doing Shakespeare with Sir John Gielgud and whenever there was a play it was in repertory form, so another play came on and I had five days off, so I'd fly to Toronto, have a three day 'loon' in Canada and then come back. Or I'd go to L.A. where David did his week's show at the Universal Amphitheatre, which was the 'Diamond Dogs' show. That was great and started a whole year of being in America for me,

which was seeing David as a major star and also for myself, experiencing life as it should be as a major star, with your cars and people looking after you and the record company being polite to you rather than treating you like shit and not working.

"DeFries gave me a fur coat. He said, 'If you're a singer, you've got to keep yourself warm'. I was really comfortably looked after — it was great. I always knew it probably couldn't last because nothing goes on forever, but in that time, I had a great time in New York, and it seemed at one point that everyone was there when David was doing the week at the Universal Amphitheatre.

"I remember we were all in the Beverley Hills Wiltshire Hotel. DeFries was in the Christian Dior suite, Marc Bolan was in the Marc Bolan suite, David was in the next one, Jagger was there and all the Stones, and every night was party night. All of the MainMan people. Most of the guys who worked for the company were gay — and Cherry Vanilla was the female press officer. . . she was outrageous. She wasn't gay but she was just outrageous. We had a great image. You only had to say MainMan or Bowie and all the doors opened. I was the first woman ever into one of the famous gay bars. I went in dressed as a man. We had a very outrageous life style — it was wonderful."

Leee Childers: "The rest of the world was handled by Tony DeFries pretty much the way America had been handled. He just decided it was time before the country had decided it was time. He certainly did that with Japan. He knew that there was a big market in Japan and that you could tour there fairly economically because it was such a small cluster of islands, and he just decided he would. I think Japan was taken by surprise. I know RCA in Japan was taken by surprise — they didn't expect a tour at the time — but he just decided to do it. And it paid off magnificently. David had no hits of any description in Japan when Tony decided to tour. He was very adventurous in that way. It didn't bother him that David hadn't had any hits — so what? Japan is there. And of course, he always got someone else to pay for everything anyway, so it wasn't any financial problem. RCA records payed for transport, so off we went. And it worked.

"At the beginning of the tour it was very luke warm. By the end of the tour, kids were throwing themselves at the stage like little 'kamikazis'. Sure it started out luke warm, but once people saw him they went crazy, and by the end of the given tour, he had a totally devoted following because he's a brilliant performer. That's what made all the craziness of Tony's orchestrations work. It wouldn't have worked otherwise. The other argument is, of course, would anyone ever have heard of David if it wasn't for Tony? Who knows?

"At that time, David was going through a period when he wouldn't fly, which was a pretty smart ploy because it gained you a lot of time between gigs, as you have to travel by some sort of surface transportation. That awful thing that so many groups get themselves involved in, when they're on a plane and they do a gig and they don't even know what city they're in, he'd manage to avoid. Now, the next gig was weeks ahead at Earls Court in London and there was a choice of sailing around the Cape of Good Hope, going over the Khyber Pass or going on the Trans-Siberian Express. The quickest and least expensive was the Trans-Siberian Express, although it was a bit of a hassle for me being an American, because Americans are not easily granted visas for Russia. It's a little easier now but in 1973. . .

"Anyway, I was told to accompany David on the

Androgeny

LLOYD/FACES
NEW
MUSICAL
EXPRESS
BOWIE
FIASCO

What
went
wrong?

HAWKWIND:
Problems
Resolved

Express if I could get a visa and off I went to Washington D.C. to apply for one and they told me absolutely not — I couldn't have one — go away. Everyone else had gone to Japan and I was still in New York trying desperately to get a visa for Russia but I couldn't get one, so I convinced Tony DeFries that if I went to Japan and went to the Russian Embassy in Tokyo, they'd be so confused by an American applying for a visa in Tokyo's Embassy that I could fake it and get one, and he said I was welcome to try. So, off I went to Tokyo and spent days in the Russian Embassy with the RCA Tokyo man, Mr Yamamoto, but still they wouldn't give me one.

"The tour in Japan was over and David left — he sailed for Vladivostok — and finally, just to get rid of me as usual (if you keep making enough noise they'll get rid of you for a little peace and quiet) they gave me a visa. At this point I had to fly and catch him up, so I flew to Khabarovsk in far east Siberia where I had to spend a night. That's where I was first introduced to the Russian system of having a 'guide' who would take care of you. She was a very nice girl named Eugena, I think, and there were guards at the end of the hotel corridors. I remember giving them the slip and wandering around Khabarovsk on my own in a snowstorm, only to be told the next day that there was quite a bit of excitement in the city during the night because a Siberian tiger had come into the city and was

▲

Top, Ziggy at the Dorchester Hotel, bottom at Heddon Street, W1. ►

◄◄

Previous pages – the view from the Trans Siberian Express of one of the typical cute Russian villages. (Insets left), Bowie on stage for the Midnight Special show and as the Goblin King from the film "Labyrinth". (Insets right), en route to record 'Pin Ups' – Summer '73.

wandering the streets at the same time I was!

"Anyway, I eventually caught up with him in Irkutsk which is in central Siberia. Now the Siberian Express is very strange. It has two classes — hard class and soft class. We were in soft class which meant you had a bed to sleep on — a sort of cot. Hard class was for the poor people, they were just on benches, but we weren't allowed in there. Much as I tried to break in several times, they always caught me and wouldn't let me in to see the poor people travelling. It's a 10 day journey with 92 stops across Siberia. David had this little compartment and used to spend his whole time in a Japanese kimono with his guitar and a bottle of this horrible Reisling wine that was full of alkaline and gave you splitting headaches, but it was all there was. So there was always a bottle of Reisling and a guitar, his Japanese kimono and him staying in bed, looking out of the window at the wolves chasing the train as we went through Siberia in the snow, whereas Geoffrey McCormack (or Warren Peace as he was known professionally) and I would get off at nearly every stop if we were awake, and run around on the platform. David didn't get off. He'd just look at us

and wave and smile until we got to Khabarovsk which used to be named Katerinberg and was the city where, supposedly, the Czar and his family were murdered. I told David that he had to get off and at least stand on the platform because it was the city where the Czar was murdered. He agreed and got dressed and we got off.

"Now on our car, as in every soft class car, we had two little girls who vacuumed the corridors and who made you tea and took care of you. Well they weren't little at all. In fact they were huge Russian girls. David had made great friends with them because they would come into his compartment at night and he would sing them songs and things. He'd take 60's songs like 'Donna, Donna The Prima Donna', and substitute their names. They couldn't understand it in English, but they'd hear their names to these kind of bouncy 60's tunes and loved David. He can be very charming in that way. So anyway, at Khabarovsk we were eating ice cream — there were always ice cream sellers on the platform — and I was taking pictures of David and sneaking pictures of the soldiers who were on the platform with us but, unfortunately, they caught me at it. The soldiers came and tried to get my camera but I was fighting back and wouldn't give it to them. David, who had a movie camera which he had bought in Japan, began to film it all. Then they got really crazy and they were trying to get David's movie camera and to arrest us all. At this point, the two girls just marched off the train, one of them picked up David, the other one picked up me, screamed Russian things at the soldiers — I haven't a clue what they were saying — and marched us back on the train and barred the door, while the Russian soldiers were standing on the platform screaming horrible things at them. The girls were screaming back as the train pulled out and we got away from Khabarovsk without being arrested.

"Eventually, we arrived in Moscow the day before the May Day Parade. David and Geoffrey were perfectly welcome because they were English, but I was not welcome because I was American, so while they were staying on to see the May Day Parade, I was meant to leave and fly to Berlin where I would wait for David and Geoffrey who were going on by

train through Poland. I decided to give the authorities the slip and went out through the bathroom window of the hotel and got myself lost in Moscow. When they finally found me it was too late to get me out, because everything stops at 5.00 p.m. the day before the parade. They were furious. David was totally horrified. He was sure I was going to be sent to Siberia but I'd given him all my film and all the pictures that I'd taken already. He was sure he'd never see me again.

"The guards and police took me completely outside the town and put me into some weird hotel that looked like a Holiday Inn, but it was in the middle of the woods. They told me to stay there until they came and got me the following day — which I didn't. I got out at 5am and left. I had with me only the name of David's hotel which was the Intourist, which was right in the middle of town, and my Russian phrase book, which was full of phrases like, 'I think my leg is broken, can you stop the bleeding?' which did not prove very helpful. I began walking towards what I thought was the town. I was in the middle of the wood, so I didn't know which way I was walking. Dawn was just breaking and I began to see a little more civilization and it looked sort of right. Then I began to run into guards, and every guard I saw, I didn't say anything, I just showed them the piece of paper, which had written on it Hotel Intourist in Russian, and the phrase book, I'd point to phrases like 'I can't see anything' or 'Has the sun come up?' and they'd look bewildered at me and point and on I'd go.'

"I made my way through all the guard checkpoints and got to the hotel Intourist in the middle of town at about 11 o'clock when David and Geoffrey were just sitting down to lunch. I walked into the cafeteria and sat down with them. David was horrified and sure that I'd be arrested and sent back to Siberia. He screamed at me and I screamed back. I wasn't about to miss the parade, and went on to see the whole event, and photographed it — all the red flags, the guns, the cannons, the missiles, everything, including Black September Group marching.

"After it was over, we went into the bar for a drink and the authorities came along. Once again, I'd given my film to David. The authorities grabbed

▲ *David and Geoffrey McCormack always travel 'Soft' class. Siberia 1973.*

me and took me away. I thought that this was it. . . Siberia for me, but all they did was put me on a plane heading for Berlin. Deported. Sickening. I'm sure I'll never be allowed back to Russia — not that I'd ever want to go back. David got out with all the film, so I have all the pictures of the whole thing."

Mick Ronson: "We toured the States followed by Japan, and by the time we came back to England, it was beginning to really snowball. I think the final Ziggy Stardust tour was in England — that was the big tour — and by the time we returned, everyone was talking about it because Ziggy Stardust was a really good show. It wasn't any deeper than that — I'm not really sure what it was — but David was very creative.

"When he was younger he'd write songs about a laughing gnome, or a song about a laughing policeman, and I think it was a great outlet for David because he could almost blow his character out of all proportion and be able to pretend whatever he wanted to pretend, which is what actors and pop stars do. You know it's a funny thing, when you get on stage in front of an audience — you become a different person and I think everybody experiences that. You get somebody who is very outrageous on stage but who is maybe very shy off stage, and I think being on stage in front of an audience enables you to step outside of your own body and be somebody else totally different for that period of time. Some people carry on and live it 24 hours a day because they have to be that person all the time and at that time, it wasn't like you played a gig, finished the gig and then had a very private life until the next gig. David would always be seen in public, would always have to do interviews, do a video or go into the recording studio — so I think the whole time was taken up by feeling involved in that whole Ziggy period or Ziggy way of thinking. You can't go into the recording studio and be Joe Bloggs. You go in there and you do what you want to do. It's an extension of what you do on stage and it became a full time thing really, until after it stopped and he could change and get into the Diamond Dogs period and the other albums that he made."

Angie Bowie: "There was a lot of garbage said about him feeling schizoid and it was all so crazy and easy to say that he felt schizoid because of Ziggy Stardust. At the time he was perfectly rational — he didn't feel schizoid — he was playing a part. A lot of actors have problems playing parts. It's easy to feel like Ziggy — of course it is — you play it on stage half the time and then you come home and have to be David Jones and I don't have too much patience for that talk. The band, for instance, they played 'The Spiders From Mars'. Did they feel like 'Spiders From Mars?' I'm sure Mick Ronson lay awake at night and worried about being like a Spider from

◀ *In Amsterdam in 1974.*

IN OTHER WORDS . . . DAVID BOWIE

Mars. It's ridiculous. It was just a good album and they played the parts really well. I suppose if one were to wonder about schizophrenia or playing the part too much, it's like an actor who does a film and the film is very successful and he plays Gatsby in the film, and then, they never stop wearing 30's tennis whites. Do you know what I mean? Basically it's all part of promotion for the period that you are filming and promoting. You may well be wearing 30's clothes and I suppose you could start wandering around feeling like Gatsby, but for a man who is a very fine actor and mime artiste, and who learned from Lindsay Kemp way before I met him, everything about it being a show off stage and on, I don't really think there's too much relevance."

David Bowie: "I ran into a very strange type of paranoid person when I was doing 'Aladdin Sane' very mixed up people, and I got very upset. This resulted in 'Aladdin' and I knew I didn't have much more to say about rock and roll.

"I mean, 'Ziggy' really said as much as I meant to say all along. 'Aladdin' was really 'Ziggy' in America. Again, it was just looking around seeing what was in my head."

After the successful tour of Japan and the trip on the Trans-Siberian Express across Russia, stopping off in Moscow to see the May Day Parade, Bowie travelled overland to Paris, and met up with Angie. By this time, 'Aladdin Sane' had been released to advance orders in the UK of 100,000, a figure comparable only to albums by The Beatles.

David arrived in London with Angie, having travelled more than 8,000 miles overland. The following day they gave a home-coming party at Haddon Hall and invited many of their friends: Tony Visconti, Mary Hopkin, Lindsay Kemp, Mick Ronson, George Underwood, Freddie Baretti, Ken Scott and Mary Finnigan whom he kissed on the cheek and said 'I love you Mary'. That was the last time she was ever to see him.

A matter of days after the home-coming party, David was back on tour, this time in the UK. The tour, opening in inglorious circumstances at London's Earls Court, marked the debut of David's new character, Aladdin Sane. It would become known as the Aladdin Sane Retirement Tour of Great Britain, comprising over 40 appearances and culminating at Hammersmith Odeon for the famous final concert of June 3, 1973, when David announced his "retirement" and that he wouldn't perform live concerts again for a long time — not for two or three years at least.

At the Cafe Royal the following night, David held a swish retirement party with guests like Mick and Bianca Jagger, Ringo Starr, Paul McCartney, Keith Moon, Britt Eckland, Tony Curtis, Cat Stevens, Lou Reed, Jeff Beck, Elliot Gould, Ryan O'Neal, Sonny Bono, Barbra Streisand, Peter Cook and Dudley Moore, with music supplied by Dr. John. By this time, nearly every newspaper had run 'I quit' stories emerging from the announcement at the Hammersmith show.

Mick Ronson: "After the tour, we recorded the album 'Pin-Ups', an album which was just a collection of songs that David really liked from the 60's period, and shortly afterwards, we went to Italy for a holiday. David wanted to write a play — that's what he fancied doing — although it never came about. That's when he actually got into the 'Diamond Dogs' period and when the show extended a bit more into the theatrical — more props with street scenes, a huge lift chair that went over the audience and things like that. I think it was a cross between writing his play and doing another rock and roll show. He really wanted to do a play on maybe Broadway at the time — something different."

Tony Zanetta, "By this time, I'd become the President of MainMan and for a time, was Tony's right-hand man running errands for him. MainMan was more about Tony than it was about David although David and Tony worked extremely well together as a team, but I think they each had individual goals they wanted to accomplish. Tony wanted an empire. He wanted to have an international entertainment conglomerate, which was MainMan. He was very taken with organization in the corporate world and MainMan was being fashioned after a large corporation although in its beginning, it was anything but that. It was basically a group of people who happened to be around but very soon we all had titles and were constantly organizing and re-organizing and creating divisions and systems and methods. Tony was always preparing for the future with David and with MainMan, so he was always two or three steps ahead of himself.

"David had come to the United States as a headliner. Tony didn't have time to waste booking him as a support act or doing a club circuit or anything like that. What happened was that we began to do all kinds of things that are normally done to support a tour that you farm out, but we used to do it in-house, so we had our own publicity department, our own travel department — we booked our own flights and our own hotels, we didn't use a travel agency. We had our own accountants in-house. We had everything. We even made our own television commercials and our own radio commercials. We also had our own publishing department. It was all fashioned after a record company. I don't know what good it did David in the long run because what it did was cost a lot of money.

"It was wonderful if you were going to service five or ten artists, but one artist didn't need all this. What it did for David was have the same mushrooming effect, creating this balloon image of star power — all that staying at The Plaza and The Beverley Hills Hotels did. It looked important. Anyone who had this kind of machine behind them must be important, so it had the effect of presenting him to the public as this bigger than life pop star which, if you look at his record sales at the time, he wasn't, but he was becoming a media myth, some of this due to his own talent and some of it due to the MainMan hype machine.

"He was talented enough and resourceful enough to survive it, although I think it almost devastated and destroyed him at a certain point. I think we all became victims of it. We acted as if we owned RCA, that we were RCA, that we had this corporation. We were very grandiose. It was really believing our own notices and becoming very arrogant. Drugs and alcohol began to creep in. There was none of this in the beginning, in the first two years, but at the time of 'Diamond Dogs', a lot of drugs began to come in, a lot of alcohol came in with different individuals, which helped fuel things. It certainly didn't help. It just added fuel to the fire. The 'Diamond Dogs' tour that followed was an enormous amount of work for everybody involved and in some ways, it began to break down.

"I really began to sense it when David did a *Midnight Special* show in 1973. What had happened was that he started doing his English Ziggy Stardust dates in early '72 and he worked without stopping until the summer of '73 when he did his Hammersmith Odeon concert and retired from the stage. When he finally did stop working, it was the first time in a year and a half that everyone involved stopped and got a chance to take a break, and once everyone took a break, things began to change.

"First of all, DeFries, by this time, had set up his headquarters in New York although David was still headquartered in London. They began to spend less time together. DeFries began to build his MainMan empire in New York and it became obvious it wasn't always in support of what David was doing. They were not in fact the same thing — they were two separate things — and up until this point, it seemed like it was all one thing — that MainMan and David were the same — but it began to become apparent that they weren't. We had a staff of 10 or 15 people in New York and there was a staff of three in London. The staff of three had to service Bowie, Mick Ronson and Dana Gillespie. All the artistes were in England, but the staff were in New York. It became obvious that something didn't make sense.

"Anyway, we recorded the Midnight Special programme at The Marquee in England and I went over and spent a month with David organizing it from the MainMan end, and the *Midnight Special* people came over from California to London to tape the show at The Marquee. Again, it was a situation where all the work was being done in London but the office was in New York, and to get money and to get certain things that we needed to do took a long time. This was the first experience where it was obvious that the machine was working against itself — something wasn't quite right.

"It didn't really become apparent until the Spring of '74 when David returned to New York to do the 'Diamond Dogs' tour. By that time DeFries had an office in Park Avenue which was very much like the old Gem offices in London. He'd made major strides in establishing the kind of company he wanted, which wasn't the kind of company that David wanted, and I think David saw that when he got to New York. Also, it had become much more formal and much more structured in organization. DeFries wouldn't drop anything anytime of the day for David any more. It wasn't exactly like he had to have an appointment, but it was that he didn't fit into the structure.

"In the meantime, I think David had come to realize that he was responsible for an enormous amount of business at RCA in the United Kingdom — something like 4% of their total gross was David Bowie products — and he was making an enormous amount of money but he didn't have anything. He didn't have any money because all the money was controlled by MainMan. Any money that he wanted, he had to ask for, or if he wanted to buy anything, he had to ask for it.

"Up to this point it had been fine because there had been no money. The money was all in a pot. It was petty cash. MainMan was always in debt and Tony had always gone out and found the money to do projects, so it was fine. I was as much a part of this as anybody. I'm not trying to be a saint in any of this at all. I still believed implicitly in Tony DeFries and I'm not trying to put Tony down by this at all. The only thing I saw wrong at the time was that David and Tony began not to communicate. Money was being spent, but money could be accounted for. It wasn't that money was being stolen or sneaked — everything was down on paper.

"David and I did have conversations about it and I told David that I thought he should get an accountant, or that he should ask for an account from Tony if he had questions about where money

◄
Final touches for a Midnight Special performance by make up lady Barbara Daley – the lady who later went on to do the make-up for Lady Diana on her wedding day.

was going. I feel that David didn't want to face it and I don't think Tony wanted to face it. They had really tired of each other and it had become a struggle between them that was slow to surface and it didn't really surface until the Diamond Dogs tour because a lot of things happened on that tour that they were both very unhappy about.

"It started with the way the tour was organized. It was farmed out to Broadway people to put together, and cost an enormous amount of money. It was a wonderful show, 'Diamond Dogs', but it wasn't practical for a tour so we all thought that if we got the Broadway experts to put it together, it would be the best thing possible — but it wasn't. They weren't used to doing this kind of thing — they weren't used

Arriving at the Cafe Royal for his 'farewell' party. ▶

to rock and roll or putting something up and taking it down every day, so really it was a white elephant from the beginning. The whole thing created a lot of stress and tension, moving this humongous thing around the country. Problems came up with musicians. DeFries was not on the road, and I wasn't on the road and I think David began to feel very abandoned by this company MainMan. He had no money and he was working very hard every day and there were lots of problems and nobody there to take care of them.

"In the meantime, he'd discovered cocaine with a vengeance. It was like his year to play drug addict. He wasn't using his best judgement. He was staying up for four or five days at a time and then crashing for four or five days. He was really living the rock star legend to the ninth degree. DeFries was very upset at this because DeFries hated drugs. They more than pulled at that point — they just stopped communicating.

"The real turning point was in the middle of the tour — the natural break in it — July and August. First of all, David did some recording in July — he recorded most of the 'Young Americans' album — and then there was break in California and we were going to restart the tour in Los Angeles. By that time, David and I had had some serious talks and I went on the road for the second part of the tour to try to salvage the relationship, which didn't really work. In Los Angeles David decided that he didn't want to use the set any more, that he wanted to change the whole concept of the show, and that, I think, was the last straw for DeFries because, as

difficult as it was as a set, it was an incredible show, quite wonderful to look at. No-one had ever done anything like that in rock and roll and it was getting incredible press. The thing about all this was that sales were beginning to meet his star image. For the first time, he was beginning to sell records in the United States, but the relationship between DeFries and Bowie had disintegrated by this time."

Leee Childers: "It all grew too fast all of a sudden. All of us had been promoted out of any efficiency that we might have had. I had a huge office on Park Avenue with a tiger skin rug, mahogany walls, a personal assistant, two secretaries and nothing to do. I used to pull the blinds, turn out the lights and sit in the dark in terror, thinking 'What am I going to do here? There's nothing for me to do. They're going to find out eventually that I'm doing nothing'. I didn't have enough experience in the music industry to be able to create any further usefulness. I could do now, with the knowledge I have, but I couldn't do it then.

"My personal assistant was my high school sweetheart, Mrs Simpson, who was a complete nutcase. She'd taken it upon herself to be in charge of merchandising, so she was working and creating little David Bowie dolls and placemats and keychains and all that shit, but she was doing that all by herself.

"Cherry Vanilla was the first to leave. To her full credit, she left of her own accord saying, 'I'm not doing anything, it's time I moved on'. And she went. I didn't. I just hung grimly on because the salary was magnificent. I couldn't dream of what I was going to do because you become so dependent on money. I talked to Tony Zanetta and he said, 'You're not doing anything are you?' I said, 'No, I think I'll go'. And so I went. I told Tony that he'd be next and he was. It was just six months later that he left.

"Anyway, having left MainMan, I came back to England and lived in Oakley Street in David's house with Angela. David wasn't there, so I was living with Angela and that's when I first got the inkling that all was not well between David and Tony. During the time that I was at MainMan, David had become more and more removed from us, but I figured that that was because he was so busy and that was the way it was when you had become a big star. It turns out, I think, that he was being purposely more and more removed from us in order to retain whatever Tony DeFries's idea was of keeping business separate from pleasure. We weren't supposed to be friends with people with whom we were doing business, which was probably a good idea, but just the same, I didn't know that until I began to live on Oakley Street and found out that David was very distressed. He thought that we had grown apart from him and he became upset that none of us were around him any more, talking to him any more. This is according to Angela who was still married to him then, and still close to him. But I found out there was trouble down at the camp.

"About that time, Tony Zanetta came to London and visited us. He was very restless so I knew it was a matter of moments before he was going to leave MainMan. In fact, he left not long after, leaving all the secretaries and personal assistants in charge, except for my personal assistant — she got fired. She told me that Tony spent a lot of the time making passes at her, but she was horribly flirtatious and very beautiful. But anyway, in the end she was fired and her last act was to send a memo to Tony DeFries, the contents of which I would rather not go into. To finish off the story, she married a millionaire in Tennessee, so she's OK."

THE AMERICAN DREAM

Tony Zanetta: "We did the last part of the tour which we called Tour Five. Some people call it The Young Americans Tour, others call it the Black Show because it was David as an R & B singer. At this point we began to work with *Carlos Alomar*. In fact, Carlos' wife, *Robyn Clarke,* was one of the back-up singers with *Ava Cherry* and *Luther Vandross*. Most of the musicians were black and the music had changed and really had an R & B flavour. The new stuff was very R & B. The opening act was the back-up singers doing a kind of almost traditional Apollo show which didn't go over. It wasn't English. It wasn't Ziggy Stardust and the reviews became very mixed.

"The tension increased on the road because David and DeFries had a very important relationship that was crumbling and one of the things about the relationship was the direction that DeFries did supply for him. You could never tell whose idea was what, because they talked everything to death, but if nothing else, DeFries was a wonderful sounding board. Maybe they were always David's ideas — I don't know whose ideas they were — but DeFries certainly was a sounding board and he would talk for hours and hours and hours about every little detail of the career and every little detail of the show, the order of the set, the music, the albums. But David didn't have that any more. Angela wasn't around very much at this point either.

"This whole experience had been so fast and furious for me I didn't know what I was doing any more. My drinking picked up incredibly. I was dabbling with drugs and doing plenty of drugs and also, I'd become very arrogant. I thought I had all the answers although I didn't know what was going on. I was trying to communicate between David and Tony, trying to get them to talk to each other, and as a result was going back and forth between the two of them which was a very frustrating experience, added to which I was tired from being on the road and was very unhappy. I suppose in a way, I was living out my own part of the Ziggy decadence and the Ziggy demise.

"We had three arrests on the tour, the third was mine. The last show on the tour was in Atlanta and I decided to give a little party for the singers and the musicians and the crew and I tried to rent a banquet room at the hotel, but because it was Thanksgiving Weekend, they said they could only give me a suite. Anyway, the party was busted by the vice squad. It was a joke really because the night detective of the hotel, this guy in his mid 20s with long blond hair who looked like a hippy with beads on, turned out to be a member of the vice squad. They had this entire set-up. It was incredible. They had undercover agents everywhere in the hotel.

"The party was the quietest you could imagine and they kept complaining that we were making too much noise. There was very little noise as no-one had arrived — between 20 and 30 people were in the room — and we had this teeny stereo system about as big as a transistor radio for music. It wasn't exactly an exciting party, but the vice squad knocked on the door. Of course, David's bodyguards were guarding the door and I went to see what they wanted and this guy, who said he was the night detective, announced that unless we emptied the room in five minutes, he was going to close the party down. He and I got into a bit of a squabble. There didn't seem to be anything to do but to close the door, which I did. Unfortunately, his foot was in it at the time I slammed it, at which point he pulled out a badge and said he was a cop. Suddenly there were policemen everywhere who ran

into the suite and made everyone get up against the wall with their hands above their heads.

"It was hilarious. Anyone who had drugs on them dropped them to the floor. Now the suite was in my name, so I was charged with possession of all these drugs, and with assault, and with a lot of other charges like operating a dive, running a disorderly house and all silly charges which were dropped the following day. But it was a fitting end to this tour. It was symbolic of the whole thing.

"When we returned to New York after the tour, David and DeFries had a couple of meetings and they were rather funny too, because I would ask each of them what happened. 'Did you resolve it? Did you settle it? Did you talk?' They each had totally different stories, totally different perceptions of what had gone on in the meetings. They each said everything was fine. By 'fine', DeFries meant everything was fine and David meant that he'd left. They were just not talking to each other at all."

Dana Gillespie: "I've got to say, I think in a way cocaine can really freeze your emotions, and David took an awful lot. I mean, everybody took loads of everything in those days but if you have an incredible tour schedule and you find a way of having extra energy, which you can get with cocaine, you overdo it if you haven't ever had it before in such huge quantities, and you're that big, and girls come to the dressing room afterwards, and everybody gives you free packets, and suddenly you're everybody's pal. Well David didn't sleep a lot and got thinner and thinner. And it makes you very hard as a person. I know because I've tried it as well, and I would say it was a large contributing factor to a breakdown of understanding, because at this point I was watching the deterioration of the relationship between Tony DeFries and David. By this time, David's show was taking on mammoth proportions — about 50 people as a road crew. The lighting guy was Jules Fisher who was the top guy in New York and then doing straight Broadway musicals, and the crew was fantastic.

"I remember there was a period when no-one was speaking to anyone and I recall going to the Island of Mustique and being there a few weeks just before the final split. There was DeFries and his girlfriend and the guy I was with and David called a couple of times. It's terribly difficult to make a call to those sort of islands as they don't have many telephones.

Wayne County and Bowie in ▲ discussion.

It takes about three days to get a call out and I remember DeFries didn't answer any of David's calls because I think he knew what was going on.

"I was blissfully ignorant of the whole collapse. I used to go as little as possible to the MainMan offices. I was aware of the fact that there had been what seemed like 20 people working in the office and then it was suddenly dwindling down to a skeleton staff. I just assumed that they were trying to cut back as they had been a bit too lavish. Not that I complained because I was having a great time with it, but I noticed that there were a few changes and when I went back to England from Mustique, that was probably the last time MainMan existed. This was in 1976. I'm sure everybody's got a different version of it and I really didn't witness any rows. I would often hear from my assistant who now looks after Cher, but at the time was delegated to looking after me, and she would say that she'd just come back from the MainMan offices and the main office door was closed into DeFries's inner sanctum and there were raised voices between David and him in there.

"I think he did once say to me that he was very disturbed at how much 'coke' David was doing and that it had got to the point where he didn't hide it in front of DeFries, whereas he did for quite a while at first. DeFries, being a straight guy, wouldn't have known what was going on. Even when he saw it being done he still wouldn't have known what was going on but unless you actually try it yourself, you don't know what physical effect, or mental effect it has on you and how speedy and intolerant it makes you of other people. It's really a sort of personality freezer. It's terrible if you take a lot of it because it's just bad for your actual personality — not for your health, except for the fact that you get thin. I saw David shovelling more and more, and as David was doing more and more, he was getting more tired, more irritable, more run-down and less able to control the madness that was going on around him.

"It was no longer just go out and do a gig with your equipment — there were lighting men, dancers, singers — there was so much that I think nobody could handle it and he was wanting more and more to make the show very good. At one point he said he wanted something and DeFries said 'No, you can't have it — you don't have the money'. I remember David had a look of amazement on his face because at this point he had quite a few gold albums, but he still didn't have the money because the rate that they made money went straight back into making the show even bigger and better, and everybody travelled in style.

"When you went out on a tour with MainMan, you did not eat in a Wimpey level of place, or stay in the Holiday Inn. Everybody had personal assistants whether they needed them or not. It was great. I had a friend, she now manages the Eurythmics with her husband, but at that time, none of us needed to be in such luxury, but none of us said no if it was offered and DeFries always observed the Noel Coward code and said, 'You should travel through life first class'. That was more or less his way of doing things and it cost a lot.

"So suddenly, David had wanted something — I don't know what it was — it might have been something like a synthesizer or some extraordinary thing for the show, but the money wasn't there. I think it was just the final end of a long line of demands that he'd been making. He wanted more of DeFries's time as well and the more DeFries saw things going on that he didn't like, the less time he wanted to put into both of them. It was a complete breakdown of a friendship in a way. I really can't answer for David because in all the years that I've known him, I always actually found him a rather cold person, even when I was 14 and he was 16, even as boy and girlfriend.

"DeFries made a lot of career decisions for David that worked, but suddenly decisions, desires to do things, were coming between the two of them, so there was a clash on whose decision was going to win and whose idea was going to win. I think David thought he was the artist and he knew what he wanted to do — which I think is actually true — the artist basically does know what he wants to do — but I think the manager should just be there to sort out the finance and try to keep you on the straight and narrow. But it was such an unusual rise to fame, a situation that apart from Elvis or The Beatles, there really wasn't anyone else to make any reference to and say this is how they got through it all, because there had been nobody else of that size who had done it, and it's hard to say how much of the rise to fame was attributed to DeFries.

"It certainly wouldn't have happened if David hadn't done the music, but it's not just as simple as that. It wouldn't have happened if Angie hadn't been around as well, to keep his morale high and encourage him. The great thing about Angie was that she was always for him, always helping him. She bought his clothes. They had the same size shoes and they wore the same clothes quite often. She was always there trying to be what he wanted and she wanted to make things great for him. At the end, he wanted to be on his own, so he'd encourage her to go out on her own and go loony with me. She became, for a short while, my personal manager — we did a radio promotion tour around England on the 'Andy Warhol' single — but I often had a feeling that they were things that were given to Angie to keep her out of David's way, to occupy her so that he could sort himself out. But all it did was to create a bigger gap that just got bigger and bigger.

"Who the rise was due to I don't know except that I think David probably wouldn't have had the idea to have opened such wonderful offices and created such a great mystique about it which MainMan had. Everything looked great from the writing paper to the T-shirts and the stickers — just everything was done well. Everyone had what they wanted. It was so great to have your personal limousine. It cost a fortune. Angie and I would ride around in a scarlet limo with a television in the back and a bar and a huge 20 stone black guy as our bodyguard in the front. It was outrageous. We dressed accordingly.

Performing a rare version of 'You Need Hands' for the Midnight Special at the Marquee club, London.

Under surveillance. three security police wonder whether to ask for autographs. ▼

Punch drunk and on tour. ▶

Angie would continuously go and buy things for David and Zowie, but also for me. All the things were designed by Natasha Kornilof or another woman called Anne Proctor, and maybe she'd make the introduction and David would meet them, but then she would follow it through and make sure the arrangements were done and the house was kept great when they lived in Oakley Street. But already in Oakley Street, he was starting to discover. . .

"The first time he ever asked me if I knew where he could get 'coke'. He said he'd just come back from Amsterdam and had tried some and said it was great and did I know where he could get some. I think it was around 1974."

Angie Bowie: "It was all so depressing. In fact I find it hard to talk about. It was really horrific. I don't know what started it because I wasn't with him. I really didn't know. I didn't understand it or share it and wasn't part of it. I just had to tend to him when it got too much for someone who is not that involved in drugs. Don't misunderstand me — this isn't the story about me, so it's not a whitewashing job. I got very involved in drugs later because I was nursing a broken head and a broken heart, but at this particular time, in 1974, I was not sophisticated about drugs.

"I'd smoked a joint and taken tincture of cannabis, which is something that I had done because I didn't smoke cigarettes, and the hippies around me would say 'Give her a spoonful of tincture of cannabis so that she'll get stoned' but I didn't know if cocaine was like that. I didn't understand the paranoia it induced. I was so concerned but I also really didn't trust other people or stupid books to explain to me whereas usually, in most things I do, if I don't understand them I'll go to the library and get books and read about it and find out. With things like art nouveau and Edwardian furniture, when David started buying them, I went and got books to get my act together in order that I knew what he was into, but with drugs, I didn't know, added to which David was very secretive and for a long time I wasn't aware that he was having a problem, not necessarily from cocaine addiction, which everybody loves to tell you is not addictive, but it is in terms of the fact that you rely on feeling up to cope — you just become more and more paranoid.

"Anyway, it was a lawyer named Michael Lipman who engineered David getting away from Tony DeFries."

Tony Zanetta: "David had moved into a little house in Chelsea in New York and called Michael Lipman. Lipman was a lawyer and an agent at CMA who were our booking agents, and we were all quite friendly. He wasn't as well known as John Eastman or Alan Klein but he was a nice guy."

Angie Bowie: "Then Michael Lipman brought a management contract — this was when we were in L.A. and David was doing so much cocaine. I'm so stupid that I started doing cocaine to try to understand him — to try to get close to him and understand where he was coming from. Can you believe anybody would be that dumb? But that's how much I loved him. I really thought that I couldn't bear not to at least understand what was on his mind, or what he was going through, but by that time my opinion was totally irrelevant — not wanted — added to which, I'm not easy to get along with anyway because I'm not a 'yes-man'. When David did things that I thought were stupid, or when he didn't turn up, or he'd turn up 'high', I told him I thought he was stupid. But I thought I was on my way out of the door anyway. It didn't take him long to realize that one less headache was getting rid of me.

"Times change. People don't always stay together. You can't expect him to be grateful for things we did together when we were in love — when we were working happily together. You can't expect a man to walk around thinking he's got to be grateful to them for the rest of his life — it's ludicrous.

"I wasn't there trying to tell him that he was doing something wrong or that he shouldn't be doing it. That wasn't the point. The point was that it basically has to come from yourself and if you feel funny about yourself, then maybe you should go to the root of what's making you feel funny as opposed to just taking downers and then taking uppers. At any time you can take too much or too little of something and die. Then no-one would have been satisfied, let alone the person who is the victim in all this.

"It only became a moot point because David was a meal ticket for so many people. There was an industry built around David Bowie. I do hope it's not the bitterness of someone who isn't logical, but sometimes it makes me emotional. I really feel for him. I feel how much he was at people's mercy, being manipulated, and it does upset me. I hate talking about it because I hate making it sound as if someone is to blame but I just can't stand people that manipulate other people. It really makes me angry."

Tony Visconti: "Prior to the split with Tony DeFries, our friendship developed once again. I was involved with the show that was recorded at The Marquee and I think a few months after that he called me and said he was doing an album called 'Diamond Dogs' and didn't know where to get it mixed. He'd been all over town and had a few vocals left, a few guitar bits, and was rather disenchanted with the studio that he was using. I had just finished building a 16-track studio in my house and asked him to come and have a go on that because it was just freshly built and I had some equipment that even the very big studios didn't have. So he brought his tapes with him that night and he loved it. It was like a little home studio but with all the big gear in it. It was everyone's dream to mix their album in the front room and that's the kind of studio it was at the time.

74

"We sat that first evening on two carpenter's benches — we didn't even have proper tables and chairs — and started mixing the album. We did a few vocals and overdubs and eventually the album was mixed bar one track, which he did somewhere else. We had all sorts of disasters that night. I did his tape copy on the machine I was using for echo and it was switched to vari-speed, so the copy was played at almost half the speed and when he got it home and wanted to play it to his friends, it sounded rather strange. But in spite of all the bumps in the beginning, he kept coming back to my little home studio and that's how the second half of our lives together began.

"I then got a phone call in the middle of the night — I always get phone calls in the middle of the night from David. He said 'I want you to mix my live album — 'David Live', so off I went to New York and we did very few overdubs, basically just the backing vocals, because the backing vocals were done by *Warren Peace* which is *Geoffrey McCormack* in disguise, and some other bloke whose name I can't remember, and as they were dancing all the time the backing vocals were rather breathless, so we had to dub them again in the recording studio. But the rest of the album, unlike other live albums, was truly live. All David's vocals were live, the band was live. I remember he had *Earl Slick* in the band then — it was a very large band, about 14 pieces on that tour."

Tony Zanetta: "I think DeFries finally realized that it was it. DeFries and David were very much alike, especially in their emotional complexion, both very cold — or maybe that's the wrong word — but neither was very expressive emotionally. What DeFries said to David or what he felt I don't know, but what he said was, 'Well, if that's what he wants, then he should leave'. DeFries was never one to tell people what to do or badger anyone. He always

expected him to leave; he expected everyone to leave. As far as he was concerned, that was where people are. He didn't think this world would last for ever and if he wanted to leave, he should leave. But what it meant to both of them was that all the money was frozen because there was a dispute over whose money was what and how much money had been spent — that was a problem for David and for Tony.

"I think it's hard to be honest with yourself about certain things and I wanted to think that I had no part in the grandiosity of MainMan and a lot of the bad things about MainMan. There were a lot of wonderful things about the organization and about Tony DeFries — he really is a wonderful man and gave a lot of people a lot of opportunities, but we all took it so much for granted. It made David Bowie a star. I'm not saying he wouldn't have become one without MainMan, but when you talk about MainMan, you have to be so definite — which part of MainMan and when. The good part, the early part, the middle part, the later part. I think it was Angie and Tony, going back to that incredible support that I told you about when I first met them, that they were also dreamers and had such faith and believed in David's future and his destiny. That was contagious you see. We were all people that were looking for something to believe in. We were all looking for some direction in our lives and they gave us that direction. I think it came from David, but Angie and Tony certainly drummed it up and sold it to us and then we went on and sold it to others. It was an ever increasing thing that blew up because it got a little too big, but it did make David a star and he has dealt with it really well, and is a man who does wonderful work. He can choose his own projects and lives a very private life. When he wants to work he does, and his work is terrific, and that's a nice way to live one's life."

◄

Candy Clarke with the man who fell to earth.

Stranger in a strange land. ▶

THE ACTOR'S TALE

F O U R

David Bowie: 'David Live' — God, that album. I've never played it. The tension it must contain must be like a vampire's teeth coming down on you and that photo on the cover — my God — it looks as if I've just stepped out of the grave, and that's basically how I felt. The record should have been called 'David Bowie Is Alive And Well And Living Only In Theory.'

In late 1974 David was still touring America. At the end of the year, he spent Christmas with Angie and Zowie in New York and by January, 1975, he had informed Tony DeFries by telegram that his MainMan services were no longer required, and that legal action had begun to free him of all existing contracts. Tony Visconti was putting the finishing touches to the 'Young Americans' album, and David was about to devote more time to his acting.

Tony Zanetta: "Having heard about this film *Nicolas Roeg* was doing, *The Man Who Fell to Earth,* some meetings were set up between Nick Roeg and David. David had been planning his movie career for a long time and on the tours he video taped everything, every single show. It was his way of directing the Diamond Dogs Show and the Young Americans show — through video tape. David is someone who is always working, always doing something. Wherever he is, whether it's in a hotel room, or in a house or an apartment. His current obsession was video and film — making movies. He was going to be a director, or that was his plan. I think he works out his problems in his work also, so he was writing his movie which I think was his way of saving himself."

Nicolas Roeg: "The script was written, and I don't usually think of who should be in something when I'm working on a script, I like to let the character develop on its own, and then, when I'd finished work on it, I thought, 'Who is Mr Newton? What does he look like?' I never have any descriptions in scripts about tall men with steely eyes. I like to let the character develop itself in a way a novelist lets a character have their own say.

"I'd seen a programme on the BBC about David which I thought was rather good and very well done, although nothing patently to do with the story I was involved with. At the time I was thinking of using, not an actor for the part, but rather a curiosity, a multi-talented human being. I liked David's work, but it wasn't that at the time that drew me to him. It was his attitude inside the programme. I liked the way he moved, the way he answered people — his attitudes had a 'mutonesque' feel to me, so I just began thinking of it and proposed it to the film company that was involved at that stage of the project. They agreed that it wasn't a bad thought although they weren't entirely convinced.

"I flew to New York to meet David. He was recording at the time and I 'phoned him and he said to come round to the house. He'd had the script beforehand and I waited for him chatting to his friends there. He was very late from the recording studio. He got back just after midnight and I thought that maybe this was a bad time to start as we were due to meet at something like 7.00 in the evening, but as he came through the door, I was

totally convinced. He was an extraordinary person, private and public. You know, very often, the public face and private man are completely different.

"We talked and talked until about 5.00 in the morning. The conversation was not completely

Negative reaction – stills from 'Just a Gigolo'.

Nicolas Roeg behind the camera (seated right).

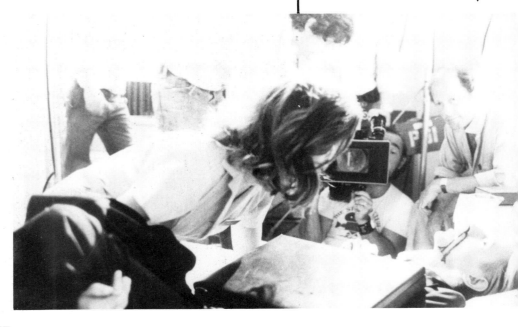

devoted to the purpose in hand — in fact, only peripherally which I rather liked and thought was rather good. It wasn't a case of talking about billing or when it's going to go or what's in it for me — it was all peripheral stuff. I suppose virtually five hours of looking at someone and saying, 'Who the hell are you? Why do you want me to do this? What's it all about? I don't know what I want to do in life.' That proved even more attractive.

"By the end of the evening (or early morning) — I only had a couple of days in New York and had to finalize things — I was virtually leaving when he said, 'I'm going to do it. You tell me when it is and we'll do it'. I said we'd obviously be in touch. I asked him if he wanted to talk about the date that we would start but he replied, 'No, no, I'll do it — that's OK'. Quite a rare thing, because one's heard that said many times in life — 'Yes, I'll do it' — then you leave someone and a couple of weeks later you get back in touch with them and they say, 'Oh, I meant to tell you love, I can't do this because. . .' But as sure as eggs are eggs, as sure as night follows day, as the date started coming up — the project was transferred from the company it was originally with to British Lion and they were rather apprehensive about not having anything completely fixed — but as the dates popped he appeared, and it was a very happy experience. Excellent in fact.

"I remember I was asked by the first company, 'Can he act?' to which I replied, 'What do you mean, can he act? Anyone who holds 60,000 people on their own in a hall — that is an act.' Their act is in fact acting and that is acting enough. I'm certain there are very few actors who can hold 60,000 people enthralled. It's odd being asked, 'Why use a singer?' He's a performing artist, not solely a singer. Conversely, nobody ever questioned whether Rex Harrison could sing when they put him in 'My Fair Lady'. He was an actor singing. Richard Harris was an actor singing. I think the whole thing is brought on by convention and wanting people in slots, and a lot of jealousy from trained actors. It's very difficult to be a completely trained actor.

"I'd describe him as someone I personally admire and my admiration is born of the fact that he never fails to interest me. He hasn't become as hard as an old walnut in terms of his beliefs and has the ability to change and surprise. That is of interest. I don't think he's rooted in, 'That's the way we always do it — they don't do it well today — if only they made movies like they did 15 years ago — rock and roll isn't the same as it was in my day — it's all finished now'. David Bowie is alive, in the present, in the future, and that is interesting and inspiring. One tends to feel, 'Oh God, why have I got to keep up.' I don't think that Bowie is by nature someone to rest on his laurels.

"The first thing that drew me to *The Man Who Fell To Earth* was that it was a man sent away, to go away and do a job, to go to a location or be working abroad and leave a family behind that he couldn't bring with him — like a refugee of a kind. But how long do you isolate yourself from the community you are in? That's what drew me to it — the isolation — the story of a man in isolation who finally has to become part of society, while not understanding that society.

"When we were working on the film, we kept on referring to the reality of this — an astronaut of inner space more than outer space. I remember David and I talking about the theme. In fact I drew an example for him of a friend of mine who had to leave the Middle East because of some affairs there and he landed in New York and couldn't bring his

family in. He was in New York for seven years and in that seven years, he inevitably fell in love with someone, but he had two small children left behind in the Middle East and they couldn't get out of the country until seven years later. He was able to smuggle letters to them and eventually they were given exit visas. He had never committed himself to, 'Oh yes, I love you and I'll get a divorce' because of the risk. He was the one that had got away and he couldn't make that commitment out of a sense of honour. It was that part of the story that I knew was quite solid and that, in reality, when it came to the point seven years later and this man had to say to the woman in New York, 'I'm leaving you, my family is coming back', they were strangers. They didn't have the chance to give, to have a chance of their relationship flowering and that was the basis of our preliminary discussions, and then to extend that in plot form, ideally within that book.

"*The Man Who Fell to Earth* was someone from outer space — an alien being, a total alien being. So, that's the basic driving thought for that. Afterwards, that element is hidden inside the film. Afterwards, it's to be enjoyed as a science fiction thing because they're all peripheral things that one develops around the basic idea. The basic premise of a man forced to be in a position where he then has to enter a society, not letting too much be known because then he'd be in continual isolation. It had to be a secret self, a secret person.

"Emotionally, I think a lot of these thoughts appealed to David. (They are) not dissimilar from many positions that many superstars find themselves in — certain amounts of isolation — not being able to be utterly themselves because once that is done, human beings have a curious pack instinct of once they're satisfied, they can put their fellow creature in a pigeon hole and that's them finished, so they must avoid being put in that hole. It's called security.

"I don't know anything about his recording business at all and I never broached it because it was an area that had nothing to do with me. It would have been only nosiness. I think it would have been impertinent and I wasn't interested. What had this got to do with the movie? He didn't bring it up at all although he did give me tickets for his concerts and, more socially than anything, I did meet Tony Visconti."

Tony Visconti: "He made the film *The Man Who Fell to Earth* and during the time he made the film, to my great surprise, he also made 'Station To Station'. It's a very odd pattern he always follows. Whenever he does an album without me, he seems to do it with the engineer I used on the previous album. He took the engineer I used on 'David Live' with him to California to do 'Station To Station'. Ken Scott, who I used on 'The Man Who Sold The World', and worked on 'Hunky Dory', the following album. I seem to be always introducing David to a new producer or engineer. It's a very odd pattern we've created in our lives.

"But anyway, he made 'Station To Station' with *George Murray, Dennis Davis* on drums, *Roy Bittan* on piano, and *Earl Slick* and *Carlos Alomar* on guitars."

Carlos Alomar: "I'd never heard of David Bowie and then he came in with his rock and roll stuff and I had been playing R & B music and had already played with Chuck Berry and James Brown and Wilson Pickett, so I had an R & B career that I had already been into, so his music didn't strike me as anything. It was just simple music. It was the mixture of rock and roll and R & B because David

always had the R & B section, but then he always layered it with rock and roll. At that point it was nice to see a mixture between rhythm and blues and rock and roll like 'Young Americans'. It was like the rock and roller going to Philadelphia to get the 'Philly' sound and bringing the New York musicians with him and trying to get everybody together so that you can get that sound. 'Station To Station' was still the same thing — funky on the bass but everything on top was just rock and roll and straight ahead.

"My relationship with David was always to take care of the music. I did see the machinery taking off and I saw it all happening, but it had nothing to do with me. My job was the music and I'd always answer directly to David and never have to worry about the machinery which was always rolling along regardless, which did create a problem because once it started rolling, it was very difficult to stop. We would just get on with our jobs and see everything that was going on, but it didn't really affect us. The decadence, fast-pacing and everything, the back-stabbing that's all business. When Tony was around, he could handle that. It was his time, his period. It was always a fast lane type of hype that was being pushed, but I was never into the fast lane that's why I've been around with David for so long.

"The first thing we did was 'Fame' with *John Lennon*. There was Lennon, Bowie and myself. It's always been that I'm playing a lick or something, or a line that he likes, and that's where we started with 'Fame'. He liked what I was playing but he didn't like the song, so he changed it and cut it up until it became 'Fame' and then I overdubbed four or five guitar parts and he liked that."

Tony Visconti: "Actually, I was at the first meeting between David and John Lennon and they were both very shy of each other. I ended up sitting up all night talking to Lennon and his then girlfriend, May Pang, because David was too shy to talk to him, but the following week when I was back in England mixing 'Young Americans', they had gone into the studio and recorded 'Fame' and 'Across the Universe'. I had nothing to do with those tapes by virtue of geography and not being in the right place at the right time. But when he did the 'Young Americans' album he was on form. It was a dream album I can tell you — having a tight rhythm section. It was fantastic doing all this live recording, 16-track, and you say, 'OK, it's a take', and they'd all play at once — no overdubs except for the odd solo. David's vocals were all live. He was down the

other end of the studio — not in a booth because he wanted to feel the band — he didn't want to wear headphones. It was unlike anything I'd ever done and the only way I could cancel out some of the noise was to use two identical microphones, one pointed towards David's mouth and the other towards his neck, one picking up his voice but the two were picking up the whole band and I'd do a technical trick by putting them 'out of phase' so that when they were both picking up the band, they actually cancelled out the band leaving Dave's vocal. There was very little spillage onto David's vocal track. Usually it's not wise to record vocals in rooms along with drums going on and pianos and electric guitars, but that's the way David wanted it and it was magic. It was one of the best albums I've ever been involved with. It was really great.

"It ended up a few weeks later in New York with a track called 'Fascination'. There were actually about three tracks that we did in Philadelphia that David didn't like, so we went back to New York and finished it, and I started the mixing in New York, but as we wanted a bit of British gloss over the whole thing, I couldn't do that in any American studios — they were not very well equipped at the time, they hardly had anything in them. Recording in America is based on the straightforwardness of the great musicians that they have there. There were no tricks. Now there are of course, but in those days you had to cut it musically and special effects were frowned on.

"So I ended up taking the tapes to my little house in Hammersmith where I still have my 16-track studio and I mixed them there. I nearly left them at Kennedy Airport en route. I bought a newspaper and left the master tapes by the cash register. I was nearly on the plane when I realized I didn't have the master tapes with me so I ran back. They were still there. No-one had dumped them in a bucket of water thinking they were bombs."

Carlos Alomar: "After that we did 'Station to Station' and that was more rock and roll. My working relationship with David was on my musical ability. I'd get together with the drummer and the bass player and we'd work on a song, maybe reggae, maybe slow or fast or up-tempo, and we'd let David hear it three or four different ways, and whichever way he wanted to do it, we just did it.

"Our relationship was based on our mutual dependence. He throws what he chooses to hear and then I give it back to him in a few ways to choose, and if he doesn't like it, there's always an endless selection of other ways to do it. That's the easiest way we work together. Basically he says, 'How about something like this?'. 'OK fine' I'd say and just start grooving and start playing until I came up with something, and that ability has been like the saving grace. Just to throw something out there and just to jam it up until it becomes a song. It's very difficult to do and it's something that he likes and that's the way David used to do all the old albums.

"He's quite good musically as far as getting ideas. His selection and choice is excellent. You see you have to have a very good knack of picking and selecting people you want to work together. It can be a catastrophe or a blessing. You pick the wrong people and they're not going to give you anything. That's another thing, when I work with David, the musicians that he gives me, I always make sure that they come through and play the way they are. I don't tell them what to play, I just direct them towards the music and he has a great knack of selecting musicians to work with each other. He's had some great lead guitarists and keyboard players, not to mention a wonderful rhythm guitarist like me. He plays a little keyboards and a little piano and sings a lot and that's basically it.

"His writing is amazing. His words are fantastic. The musical part of it — it's all right but it doesn't kill me, partly because I'm to blame, but that's what he wants. The writing is excellent and comes from scattered bits. What I mean is that he has different methods to construct a lyric which is rather nice because you don't get blocked. They can come in free verse or they can come in cutting up little notes to himself and putting them all together, or free rhyme; anything but a limerick. He's very good at writing a song and quite fast too, especially when he's doing an album. He won't let up until it's done. That's all you have to think about when you're doing an album — 24 hours a day. You dream it, you sleep it, and you eat it.

"David actually takes less time than most. When we first started doing albums, he was used to two or three months with the Spiders From Mars and stuff like that, but when we did the 'Young Americans' album it took two weeks to record the rhythm section and probably another week or two to mix, so that's a month in all. Usually it's completed in a month which is extremely fast. Once the ideas start flowing, you don't want to block it by taking too much time off — only for the mix do you really take time off. The actual construction of songs and putting them down should only take two or three weeks, but the mixing — well, that can take for ever.

"To me, David had two great highlights. The first was in 1974. At that point I was in awe of just seeing the machinery take off. Bowie, the underground psychedelic kid, suddenly became morning music kind of guy because at this time, in 1974, 'Fame' had been released, and that was the first time that he had bridged going to AM as he was always FM, and at that point, just everybody was watching in awe as suddenly the mystique and everything took off. Once the machinery started going, then it was a little bit more difficult. 'Who is David Bowie?' Suddenly he's associated with everybody and yet, who is this man?

"The first word I would use for David is calculating. You're talking about a calculating, pensive, intelligent man. You're not talking about somebody who's thinking about what he wants to do — you're talking about somebody who knows what he wants to do, and everything is pretty calculated. I don't mean that to sound cold. It's just that there are reasons for everything and that he's looking for

reasons now, so I would describe him as being a little calculating. He is sincere, as far as it's possible when you become a mega-superstar, but all of that is just based on associations with who you can use and who you can't. In the beginning he was very dear, very vulnerable. He was more sensitive and he could break down. You know, 'Don't tell David about. . .' — that type of stuff — but now, he'll yell back at you whereas before he'd sneak away and just bite his lip. He was very much like that before; he was very vulnerable. He'd say things like, 'Was that OK?' or 'How was that?' At the time, we were all vulnerable because we were hoping that it would catch. Now it's caught."

By late 1975 filming on *The Man Who Fell To Earth* was complete and the final cuts were being edited by Nicolas Roeg at Shepperton. With the completion of the 'Station To Station' album, rehearsals began for a new world tour which would open in February of the following year.

David flew to Jamaica to meet up with the rest of the band, but on his arrival he found that no arrangements had been made for his stay there. Michael Lipman, who by this time had taken over management from Tony DeFries, was promptly fired by David.

In February, 1976, the new world tour opened in Vancouver without the traditional entourage that MainMan had developed. Many of the extravagant trappings had been dispensed with, and presentation was reduced to a minimum. With Michael Lipman's departure, Patrick Gibbons, formerly the tour manager on the 'Diamond Dogs' tour acted as manager though David maintained overall control with his personal assistant, Corinne 'Coco' Schwab.

During the European leg of the world tour Bowie was held at the Russian/Polish border following a trip to Moscow. Customs confiscated Nazi books that were in his possession.

David Bowie: "I'm working on a film on Goebbels and they found all my reference material," David was later quoted as saying by New Musical Express. (No such film ever materialised).

David Bowie: "The whole 'Station To Station' tour was done under duress. I was out of my mind totally — completely crazed really, but the main thing I was functioning on was, as far as the whole thing about Hitler and rightism was concerned, mythology. I had found King Arthur. It was not as you probably know. . . I mean, this whole racist thing came up quite inevitably and rightly but, and I know this sounds terribly naïve, but none of that had actually occurred to me insomuch as I had been working, and still do work, with black musicians for the last six or seven years and we'd all talk about it together — about the Arthurian period, about the magical side of the whole Nazi campaign and the mythology involved."

In May the world tour arrived in the UK. There is a notorious picture of David waving to fans at Victoria Station in which he appears to be making a Nazi salute. He was furious at this allegation. The tour concluded with six dates at the Wembley Empire Pool after which David and Iggy Pop left for a vacation at the Château d'Herouville in France. That was the intention but instead work started on Iggy's album 'The Idiot'. A few months later Carlos Alomar, Dennis Davis, Ricky Gardner, George Murray and Roy Young, along with *Brian Eno* and Tony Visconti, arrived at the château to start work on David's new album 'Low'.

Tony Visconti: "This began the electric period of our lives. We were both fairly grown up and had both achieved success. David phoned me up one day and said, 'Look, I'd like to make an experimental album. I'm really tired of doing what's right, what's commercial and being one step ahead. I've got a great idea. I've met up with Brian Eno and would like you to give up four weeks of your time. We might not even release it, but I'd like you to come to France where I've booked the Château d'Herouville and I'd like you to do some work with me and Brian and just see what happens'. I said, 'That's fine, I've got a few toys, a few new gadgets'. I had a few ideas that I wanted to try as well and I think it was about a week later that I went. At the time, David wanted me to get a guitarist for him. He was always changing guitarists like we change socks, and I got this guy called Ricky Gardner who I'd been making some demos with and he was one of the best guitarists I've ever worked with. We started churning out these strange songs for 'Low'. We were using the band that we had used on 'Young Americans'. It was George Murray on bass, Carlos Alomar on guitar, and Dennis Davis who played on 'Fame' and 'Fascination'. We had once again a very unusual band.

"The Château was a very unusual place. I'd been there about three times before but this time the talk at dinner every night seemed to be about the ghosts that haunt the place. The atmosphere was getting worse and worse. Apparently the ghosts of Frederick Chopin and George Sand haunt the place because they lived there for a long time. There was the master bedroom which was George Sand's bedroom that David had, although he wouldn't sleep in it. There was this beautiful bedroom going to waste so I ended up sleeping in it, and I can tell you it was haunted. There was a dark corner of the room that even if you shone a torch in the corner, it sucked the light into it. It was very eerie and there was an adjoining door which went to the next bedroom. It was like in the middle of the night, George Sand used to sneak into Chopin's bedroom — that's where the psychic activity was. I'm telling you I didn't imagine this. Also, there was another bedroom in the back where Brian Eno slept and every night he was woken up by a tap on the shoulder or a voice in his ear. We just seemed to bring it out of the place.

"As I said, I'd worked there before with *T Rex* and nothing like that had ever happened, so we had this sort of eerie thing happening and I think David is quite a psychically charged person — there's no denying that. Also, he was leaving a manager at the time and also leaving Angie and Michael Lipman — he was absolutely morbid. There were very rare periods when he was up and very excited — those

moments were definitely captured on tape and he would go in and do a backing track, but this would be followed by long periods of depression and by frequent trips to Paris where he had to meet his lawyer about the split-up with Michael Lipman. It was a very upsetting time.

"I think this was the beginning of David distrusting people; not sure that it was good to have his friends around him. It looked like he made friends with all these managers and in the end they just turned round and put a dagger in his back. David definitely got the feeling that he was being ripped off. He even grew a bit suspicious of me at one point although he had no cause to because I was one of the people who was keeping him sane on that album, and as a result got very close to him. I was with him night and day just trying to keep his head above water because he was really sinking — he was so depressed.

"All the experiments were going fine when the three of us were in the studio. It was really hot. Brian Eno and David and myself were really creating some magic there, especially the second side where we were doing all this dreamy synthesizer music. It wasn't being done, apart from Tangerine Dream, and what Brian Eno had done, ambient music and 'Music For Airports' and all that, but we were going to expand this. We were doing it very well, but it was always interrupted by David's legal and personal problems and there were some ugly incidents on that album.

"Angie actually sent her boyfriend at one time — I can't remember his name — to cheer David up. I wouldn't exactly call that cheering up your ex-husband by sending your present boyfriend. Anyway, they had a punch-up in the dining room and started throwing bottles around and I remember going in there and tearing them apart. There was one afternoon when David just went comatose after he'd had a horrible meeting with Michael Lipman — he just went pale and wasn't good for about three days and we just called the recording sessions to a halt. It was a very, very sad period and I had to do what was right. I just stood by him and hung on in there and we eventually got the album finished.

"Another thing was that we were working with a skeleton staff at the studio as a lot of them were on holiday and for the first week we were eating frozen rabbits without any vegetables. I remember the night we finally complained and they actually gave

The Oblique Strategist – Brian Eno, David's collaborator on 'Low', "Heroes" and 'Lodger'.

▼

The Duke in Europe.

us a few heads of lettuce. It was the worst service I've ever had in a residential studio. We finally found a studio in Berlin called Hansa where we would eventually mix the album and to this day, the studio in France denies that we were poorly treated. We only have about 12 witnesses to the fact that we were but you know the French — you know how they are — they deny everything. It was awful that period. It was the worst album of my life, the logistics and atmosphere. In the end we quite rightly called it 'Low' and made a lot of money out of it, so screw it."

Brian Eno: "The fact that I was on that album indicates that Bowie was ready to make some kind of change anyway, so he invited me along knowing that I probably implied the direction that he was interested in. It would be quite wrong to give the impression that he was a kind of passenger being carried along by it, but I certainly applied pressure in a direction that I thought was interesting which was more instrumental, a stranger sort of direction — you know, the darker side of that record was of interest to me. I think the cover note credits are quite accurate in terms of what I did physically on the record, the other things are unquantifiable anyway. You never really can tell what somebody does spiritually to a record.

"It came at a time when it was quite a familiar form of experimentation to me. From 'Another Green World', which was one of my albums, onwards I'd been working with material that was similar to that and I'd been trying to work out more ways of using the studio and new ways of composing with the studio which I think, at the time, were quite revolutionary although I don't think they are now. I think they've become commonplace, or relatively, but at the time, they were new approaches to using the studio. My conception was not that you took into the studio a mental piece of music which you then tried to form physically, but that you went into the studio and you began working there exactly like a painter begins working on a canvas. You start with tabula rasa, a white sheet, and you put on tints and take things off and add new things. It was a very impressionistic way of working which I think was quite unfamiliar to David but which he also had liked in my previous work.

"I feel all the limitations that one approaches a piece of work with can be regarded as the skeleton of the work, so the fact that I have several limitations as a musician, the fact that I have some strength as a musician, the fact that there was a particular group of people involved on that record (Tony Visconti was also very, very important on all of those records), those all become the skeleton of the piece and putting on the flesh is really interesting as long as you understand the nature of that skeleton. You run into problems when you try to put on flesh that is not supported by the skeleton; it just won't stay on or bones stick out or whatever, and you have to grasp the anatomy of a situation and its social anatomy, a technical one, an aesthetic one — it operates on lots of different levels — and I think I had a fairly good grasp of the anatomy of both things because they weren't so different from what I'd been working on anyway myself, and I wasn't frightened at all the prospects of sitting in the studio and not knowing what was going to happen or what was going to come out at the end of the day.

"Whether or not his personal problems and business problems affected his mood when he was working is a different question. It meant that he was distracted some of the time, especially on the album 'Low', which for me was not a bad situation because it meant that I had a chance to work alone on the music and since we didn't, at that point, know each other very well, working alone had a certain value to it. It meant that I could take a thing as far as I wanted in my direction and then offer it and say 'If you like it, that's fine' — and he usually did like it — so it had a useful effect on me. It opened up a space for me to work in and having proven myself in that space, then in future we worked quite comfortably together I think."

Tony Visconti: "We started churning out these strange songs for 'Low'. We were using the band that we used on the 'Young Americans' — George Murray on bass, Carlos Alomar on guitar and Dennis Davis. Dennis was used on the latter sessions of 'Young Americans' when Andy Newmark and Willie Weeks had to go to other engagements. We again had a very unusual band, including a guy on piano who was really big around The Beatles time in the 60's and lived in Hamburg."

Brian Eno: "There were different musical talents and one of them is the talent of being a cook and a chef with other people's talent. I think James Brown is that kind of musician as well. I don't know if James Brown plays all the instruments at all, I don't know what he does, but he does sing. I don't think he writes his songs particularly. I think he watches what his musicians are doing and he somehow creates an atmosphere that brings very good performances out of them. He watches those performances and selects from them and says, 'A bit of that, a bit of that, a bit of this, drum fill, a bit of that guitar lick,' and he has a new piece. Now people sometimes say he's just living off the talents of his underlings but the point is that those musicians often don't recognize what they're doing themselves. I've often worked with musicians who can throw out 150 great ideas a minute but are unable to select from them and concentrate on one and make it into a piece of music because ideas aren't pieces of music you know — they're just licks or riffs and to make something solid requires a talent that I think Bowie certainly has, the talent for spotting things in other people. He's a kind of collagist. He thinks, sometimes successfully, sometimes not successfully, but on average quite successfully I think. He realises the combination of this talent with that talent will be something interesting and can often make the two work together, so he understands the anatomy of the situation which is something I think I'm also good at and I do like collaging different talents together.

"I think it's something that jazz composers knew about. I'm sure Duke Ellington was a great example of that kind of skill as well, of knowing that a particular group of instrumentalists would trigger each other.

"Dennis and the lads, Carlos and George, were so important, so overwhelmingly important that they should be mentioned frequently and in big letters, because they really provided the seed for a lot of things. What would quite often happen was a chord progression would be offered to them. Now chord progressions are ten a penny, there's nothing special about them, but they would keep kicking that around until they had something that resembled an arrangement. This would usually be such an interesting arrangement, because they're such good musicians and so inventive with rhythmic approach,

that within an hour or so they would have something that sounded like a song from being given a set of chords.

"Now, of course, frequently, there wasn't a song in existence. There was no lead line, there was no lyric; there was literally just a chord sequence. Sometimes it was a very fragmentary chord sequence as well. It would go C here, D, G — C, D, G, — no, make that an A. It was very negotiable up to a certain point. They would keep working on it with not very much intervention from anybody else. They really developed that stage on their own. Then David, and sometimes Tony and sometimes me, would say, 'That's an interesting idea, let's fasten on to that for a while and keep that one going and work other things around it'. So, those guys deserve a lot of credit.

"Anyway, having done that part of it, they wouldn't be that much involved in what happened afterwards, except for Carlos. His initial guitar part would get the song together but he would usually put a second one on which was the real guitar part and work with the other one. That's the easy part to describe. After that it becomes more nebulous because then there would be a lot of experimentation. It would take the form of maybe David experimenting with keyboards or other instruments. Me, I'd often be treating things while the musicians were playing. Anyway, I was trying to give some kind of sonic character to the track so that the thing had a distinct textural feel that gave it a mood to begin with, and there'd be quite a lot of that going on. It's hard to describe that because it was never the same twice and it's not susceptible to description very easily in ordinary musical terms. It would just be doing the thing that you can do with tape which is that you can treat the music as malleable. You have something down there but then you can start squeezing it around and changing the colour of this and putting this thing much further in front of something else and so on, and that would be stage two and quite a lot of that was going on.

"Stage three usually would be, if I remember correctly, the generation of a song of some kind which David would often do by performing in front of the mike singing quite freely, at which he is extremely good, as several good singers are. He is confident of his vocal range and has many vocal guises that he can slip into, and it was quite interesting hearing him experiment like that — moving from one kind of emotion in his voice to a different one and finding by experiment the dominant emotion of the song, finding the voice that fits the sound. Poor singers can't do it, they only have the one voice, but he has plenty of voices.

"Once he'd found the voice for the song, it seemed to me the melody would fall into place and the lyrics would start appearing. Sometimes, quite often I suppose, later on, Tony and I would be somewhat involved in the vocal process of saying, 'Let's go back to that idea you did on that track (this would be on many simultaneous tracks) and try putting this idea with this one — this approach seems interesting — there's some kind of tension between this type of voice and that one', and we'd be commenting, but it was mostly very much David's show more than any other stage of the recording.

"There was a certain grandeur to the recording sessions of 'Low' and the album that followed it. There were people arriving from New York and Switzerland and from London. A whole crowd would turn up. It was rather a big event. The actual beginning of recording was exciting — there was a celebratory feel, at least on those two records."

Tony Visconti: "Another thing happened shortly after the album was finished. . . Tony DeFries suddenly arrived and still purported to be David's manager. RCA complained that there weren't enough vocals on it and DeFries said he'd get him to put more vocals on it. One guy in RCA said he'd buy him a house in Philadelphia so he could make another 'Young Americans'. We were getting such adverse criticism from the record company, so David just looked at the small print of his contract which read that they had to put it out. He took a very great risk on that album and although it wasn't a big seller, I've got a gold record here somewhere, so it must have sold over a million. It was very adventurous and I'm very proud of it. It was the beginning of the Berlin period.

"At the time, David's life was being handled very well by *Coco,* there's no question about it. She's known as *Corinne Schwab* but Coco seems to have stuck. I remember the first day she showed up. She was a typist in the MainMan pool. David had another personal assistant who was not doing very well and so they just pulled Coco out of the typing pool. She came when we were doing 'Diamond

Dogs' and made coffee the way he liked it, and served him well. She became indispensable after a period of a year or so. I know Coco has been described as a very domineering person. She's completely taken over the logistics of his life. I don't know if he honestly knows how to dial a phone any more because Coco does everything for him. You can't get to him until Coco screens you on the phone. It's very difficult for me now to even phone him up. All I can tell you is that at the time his life was a mess and Coco straightened it out. He got what he wanted from her."

Leee Childers: "Corinne Schwab, believe it or not, really and truly was born in Bloomingdales' linen department where her mother went into labour. Anyway, towards the end of MainMan she was more or less the office manager in the London office. She was running things and, for reasons which I could never figure out, she really turned on Tony Zanetta and was horrible to *Tony Ingrassia.* She was real nice to me I hasten to add, and has remained nice to me to this very day, but she seemed to pick people that she didn't want to have anything to do with David, or to have any influence on David, and would openly go for the throat and

get rid of them. She was doing it even then though she had no real influence over David at all, but I think it appealed to him — that sort of approach, that sort of fierce protectiveness. He used to encourage jealousy amongst us to see who was closest to him so I guessed Corinne particularly appealed to him because she made no bones about it. She went right after it.

"So she grew in favour until she decided she was strong enough to take on Angela and she did, openly. Openly defied Angie for David's affections and David's favour. Well the problem with Angie was that she was always David's equal, even his superior artistically on occasion, and that had always made him insecure, but now he had a girl who was wildly ready to grant him superiority on every level, **and wanted the position of his confidant — and defy** the world on his behalf as opposed to his wife Angie who was not willing to grant him any of that. She wasn't giving ground just because he was famous. She knew him. And that's an old pattern with people who become famous. They often like to get rid of the people who knew them when they weren't famous because they know the vulnerable side and it's a link to the past that generally gets discarded

along the way when you become very famous.

"It was an easy battle for Corinne. It was easy to achieve prominence over Angie at that time and the funny thing is, she remained very, very friendly to me. Told me that her new name was Coco, showed me her new glamour pictures taken by — what's his name, the one who did the 'Young Americans' album (Eric Stephen Jacobs) — he was a good photographer anyway and he did pictures of her. She showed me the pictures and told me she was Coco and she was now the power to deal with as far as David was concerned. I thought it was all a little amusing at the time and it turns out she's even more than that. She's completely the wall around David now so it's really an American success story. Little girl born in Bloomingdales' linen department, more or less on her own in England, answers an ad for secretarial help and now she is, to all intents and purposes, in charge of millions and billions of pounds and is the only person to deal with if you want to reach David Bowie.

"She's achieved much more than her ambition I'm sure. A very odd woman and still, to my knowledge, has not been evil to me. But she will after she reads this. But it is the truth. She's an odd creation of show business — one of those people who achieve power for nothing. Nothing to offer except to be the security between the star and the rest of the world, so you can take it, turn it to your own advantage and you become Coco."

Angie Bowie: "David's accountants in Los Angeles had decided that there was not very much that they could do because as far as they could tell, David's tax situation was in such a mess that taking residency in America would have resulted in enormous tax bills, so I kept saying 'Let's go to Switzerland'. I was told that the lawyers had already investigated Switzerland and it was an area that had closed up giving residency permits. I pointed out that I was at school there and it's totally different what they tell you on the 'phone in Switzerland to

Conversations in Japan. ▼

what you hear in America. I knew how to get residency in Switzerland and I said I'd deal with it. I said to David, 'Do you want me to go on this tour with you or do you want me to go to Switzerland and get residency, because everyone seems to be at a loose end regarding this tax?'. 'OK', he replied because he knew that I was well connected in Switzerland and wouldn't have a problem there at all.

"So anyway, I arrived in Switzerland and the first thing I did, after checking in at the hotel, was to call my old school and then went to meet the new headmaster which was followed by lunch with the headmistress, the treasurer and the vice president of the French side of the school. I then got the names of the attorneys, phoned up my old friends in Lausanne and got the name of their attorney and their parents' attorneys. I then went to see all three of them and explained exactly what I wanted; the one that said 'Yes', I went with.

Corinne 'CoCo' Schwab. ▶

"I arrived there in February and by April, Marion, our Nanny, and Zowie came over, by which time it was done. In all it had taken about four or five months. I'd found the 'cuckoo-clock' house — my lovely house — and our stuff was moved from London and we moved in. All the time this was going on, David was touring and touring and touring and touring, but he got to Switzerland in time for Zowie's birthday. He had a big birthday party at the Casino de Montreaux, which was fabulous, and videoed the children doing a 'thematic' representation of Jack and the Beanstalk. David and I had a terrific time because we went and got all these instruments and put them there for the kids. David was fabulous. He's so good at that. He loves

that street theatre and improvisation with kids — it was terrific. We have a wonderful video of them doing Jack and The Beanstalk with David narrating and the kids acting all the parts — it was terrific.

"It wasn't long after this that David decided that the last person he could talk to or have anything to do with was me and it was at this point that he went into hiding. I received a message that he was having a nervous breakdown and that Corinne Schwab's family were well connected in the psychiatric field in Switzerland and that he was going to go to Zurich for treatment but in the meantime he couldn't speak to me or have anything to do with me. To add to this, at the same time, all the attorneys had arrived for the Michael Lipman lawsuit and were holed up on Vevey waiting for him to recover, so the whole situation was dreadful."

Tony Visconti: "It seemed Angie had become a constant source of pain to David. In the beginning Angie was performing the same service as Coco is now. She used to sort out the logistics of his life. She used to dress him up. She gave him lots of courage. But there was a time, undeniably, when it all went sour and of course, Angie was going to want to get rid of Coco but I think the harm was already done. I don't think Angie could have possibly changed the course of time. All the pain, the bitterness that went on. I didn't witness this, but I could see it in David's eyes when he spoke about it. Also, I was asked to be a character witness against Angie in David's divorce case so that he could get custody of Zowie, and that's exactly where my loyalty is. I had to sit in the dock and say whether I thought Angie was a fit mother or not. Obviously I said 'no' and that was how I felt at the time. I haven't seen Angie for years so I don't know if she's a fit mother now or not. I'm sure she is.

"Anyway, of course, she wanted to get rid of Coco but I thought it was too late at the time. Coco was doing marvellously well for David. She made him happy. She kept the irritating people out of his life and Angie had become one of them."

Angie Bowie: "Another incident which took place in Berlin before I left was that David was taken ill. It was understandably diagnosed as an anxiety attack. At the time, being a youngster, I considered that he must be having a heart attack at least. But he was having an anxiety attack because Corinne wouldn't . . . first of all she wouldn't come home —

she wouldn't come back to the apartment. She was staying with friends. She was miffed because I was in Berlin and I wouldn't agree to have anything to do with him unless he got rid of Corinne — so he had an anxiety attack but I thought it was a heart attack. I took David to the hospital — it was very exciting in the middle of the night calling up the hospital and all that. He was alright. He was fine in the morning, once he could get away from all the things that were pecking at his brain — poor thing.

amazing city, I love it.

"Iggy Pop was living with David. It was a great place. They were three calm people. Every time I saw them, I had a feeling there was an aura of calmness around. It was a wonderful period.

"I remember one night David said 'I still get recognized in the street and I wish I could just walk around here and enjoy myself'. So, I gave him a crewcut — being Italian I always carry barbers' scissors with me you know. I sat there and gave

◄
Bowie fades to grey – a still from the 'Ashes to Ashes' video.

"I guess David was dealing with two or three things at that time. He was dealing with legal battles which had to be fought, the album and his own head. Those were the priority of things he was doing. I was in London working.

"Then I got mad and I left. I tried to burn Corinne's room with vodka — I thought vodka was totally flammable like petrol — so I took all the clothes that I'd ever bought for her and given her and made her get so that she looked beautiful — you know, good looking enough to be going anywhere — to be seen in the same room as David. I piled them all in the middle of the floor and put vodka on top of them and tried to light them, but they wouldn't light because it wasn't flammable. So then I got mad and threw a bed out of the window onto two parked cars.

"After that, I took a PanAm flight out at 6 o'clock in the morning. By this time David had told me how much he loved me, gone to meet his girlfriend, and Corinne Schwab had run away to stay with her friends. So they had their secret little rendezvous and I just had to get on a plane because I thought 'No more'."

Tony Visconti: "Life was simplified. Gone were the big limousines. David was down to one car and he lived in a fairly simple flat in Berlin. It had about five bedrooms but he never filled it with furniture. He had a room dedicated to his painting and Coco lived in a flat downstairs in the same block of flats. It was in a poorer section of Berlin, but really arty. I think every section of Berlin is arty — it's such an

David a very close cropped hair cut and at that time he was already growing a moustache. I was in Berlin because we were mixing Iggy's album, 'The Idiot' — I came in on the tail end of that one. So anyway, then I gave Iggy a Mohican hair cut. He just wanted it cut slightly closer on the sides but I cut it so close that he had patches of bare skin showing at the side and he said 'Go all the way' and I shaved the sides of Iggy's head. They just did not look like David Bowie and Iggy Pop. I think I've got maybe one or two pictures from that period.

"I remember the four of us going around Berlin in a car. We went to East Berlin across Checkpoint Charlie where you have to show your passport to the East German police. David's passport had a picture of him with curly hair from his 'Space Oddity' days and Iggy Pop had platinum blonde hair in a Beatles hair cut. The guards took one look at it and burst out laughing at the two passports. David and Iggy were holding back their aggression and gritting their teeth saying, 'Very funny'. After the guards had a good laugh they let us in and we drove all around East Berlin all day. We went to museums and had dinner at the British Consulate in a restaurant next to the Brecht Theatre, and this began David's fascination with Brecht and Kurt Weill as well.

"It was a great period. There was a lot of calmness, a lot of peace in his life. He was settling down and Zowie was with him a lot. He went to school in Switzerland but at weekends he would come back to the Berlin flat with the Nanny, Mary, and he was very happy in that period.

"We finished Iggy's album, 'The Idiot', in Hansa Studios in Berlin and I came back again and did 'Heroes' there, which is probably the total reverse of 'Low'. It was the best, most positive album that we'd made together. We just couldn't do any wrong. It was a very happy time and the album just went like magic. Everybody played well on it. There were no bad scenes. The vocals were still being written on mike — David never stopped that — and he never had a clue what he'd sing about until he actually walked in front of the microphone. But by this time I was used to it and it was no longer a nightmare for me — it was fun. He was the only person I could work with who was like that. I remember once telling this to someone else I'd worked with and it took him eight hours to write a vocal on mike. He finally came out of the studio to listen after the eight hours and admitted it wasn't very good. It was only David who could really do this.

"Anyway, I mixed 'Heroes' at Hansa and then I went to New York and cut it. It was the first time I actually saw David socially. I would go back to Berlin just to hang-out with him. We went back to square one where we used to hang out together when we first met and I totally loved the city — it was fantastic.

"Berlin is so small. Everywhere is near The Wall. It's basically a small city that's divided into two, so you're never very far from The Wall wherever you go. David lived in the section where the Turkish immigrants live. You can get a very big flat very cheaply — I suppose like Islington in London. It only took us about 15 minutes to get from his flat to the studio which was about 500 yards from the Berlin Wall. From the control room we could see The Wall and we could also see over The Wall and over the barbed wire to the Red Guards in their gun turrets. They had enormous binoculars and they would look into the control room and watch us work, because they were as star struck as anyone. We asked the engineer one day whether he felt a bit uncomfortable with the guards staring at him all day long. They could easily have shot us from the East, it was that close. With a good telescopic sight, they could have put us out.

"He said that you get used to it after a while and then he turned, took an overhead light and pointed it at the guards, sticking his tongue out and jumping up and down generally harassing them. David and I just dived right under the recording desk. 'Don't do that', we said because we were scared to death. It was a really bizarre situation for people like us who are not conditioned for that sort of thing. It was a bizarre situation making a record that's eventually going to be on everyone's turntable in a few months, and you're doing it in front of Red Guards with

Pensive in Paris. ▼

machine guns and binoculars and barbed wire. But I suppose we rose above that situation and that's why the album was called 'Heroes'. We did get very heroic about it. I suppose it was like a heavy confrontation for us which we came through. It was really great.

"Everywhere you go in the city there are bombed-out buildings next to brand new buildings. They keep the bombed-out ones — although they could easily afford to get rid of them — as a memento of the war, of the Berlin invasion, of the state of the city. The East of Berlin was less bombed-out. They've built it up more quickly and there are more things preserved. West Berlin is really devastated but there are also very beautiful places. There is the Wannsee Terrassen. It's restaurant in an area called Wansee and it's where Hitler used to go for his summer holidays and all that and the SS used to go there. It's a very beautiful lake in a park area and that part of Berlin is extremely beautiful.

"David was always pursuing Hitler's haunts for some reason and we always found ourselves where Hitler was. It was fascinating to know that Hitler had been there. You know, we were sitting in a seat in a restaurant where he ate. An unusual experience.

"The other Berlin we pursued was at night. The nightclubs there are very bizarre — really truly amazing. We went to one club where Marlene Dietrich started out. She used to sit on a stool dressed in a tuxedo with a top hat, similar to the stuff she used to do in her later movies, but she used to do it for real as a 19-year-old singer. Anyway, we went to this club and it's now run by transvestites. It's a gay club. Not gay in the sense that it's a pick-up place — it's a very respectable transvestite review. You see all these old guys about 60 years old dressed up as women. They looked really fantastic, really great. They do cabaret acts very much like you've seen with Liza Minelli and like Marlene Dietrich in her films only the guys do it. There's no stage, it's done on the floor and there's a smokey mirror where you can see the backs of the artistes while they entertain. It's the same mirror that was there back in the 1920s, all preserved and intact, even the velvet seats we were sitting on.

"We found this out because we met a 75-year-old art dealer who'd been going there and living in that area since the Dietrich days. He claimed to have slept with her but I suppose there's always one. He was a fascinating man. We met him on a few occasions and he told us the history of the place which was absolutely intact. In fact, there were no other buildings in use in that street. We used to go there quite often just for the atmosphere — it was like a speakeasy. We went to the door and a little peep-hole would open and you'd see an eye come to the peephole and hear a voice say 'Ja'. We'd say that we had a reservation for four in the name of Jones and the door would open and it would be a bloke in a dress. They made no attempt to disguise their voices. We used to have a real ball there, get drunk as lords and go home, and then to studios the next day and talk about it.

"There was no particular reason that we were going to the gay clubs except that they were the most entertaining. There was another one run by a tall man/woman/transvestite/sex change, I'm not sure which, called *Romy Haag*. She was about six feet tall. Her cabaret was on a stage about ten feet wide and she used to have as many as twenty people on that stage all doing these quick vignettes. They'd put strobe lights on and it looked like old fashioned movies and then they'd mime to the records. I

Hansa Studios by the Wall, Berlin.
◄

remember Romy herself did a great mime to one of David's records, 'The Port of Amsterdam', but it was speeded up so that the voice was in a female range. It was quite bizarre and you felt like you were in a Fellini film.

"All the contemporary German musicians were coming to the studio or we'd meet them socially. It's a small city and a city which gives large government grants to artists. If you're a musician and want to set up a studio, the government will pay for the whole lot; if you paint, they'll buy a studio for you. A lot of industry left Berlin leaving behind these enormous warehouses and lofts and the government will gladly give you money to set up a business there. Geographically Berlin is cut off from the rest of free Germany by about 150 miles so you have to travel through Communist territory to get to a free island in the middle of East Germany, and there's always this impending doom that those walls will come tumbling down any minute, those big tanks are going to come through the street. The West Germans have their own big, black tanks that look like Darth Vader Starwars tanks and every day you see at least one of them in the streets. They're nothing like the World War Two tanks you've seen. They're slick, black instruments of death and you see them every day in Berlin and get the feeling, after a while, that it's going to end any minute. The so-called truce, the so-called peace is going to end any second. That's why it's an amazing city to work in for all those various conflicting reasons. It's very decadent, but on the other hand, there's a lot happening — it's very alive. You are consciously aware when you are in Berlin of what's going on and you don't fall asleep in that city. It's like a 24 hour city."

Angie Bowie: "I didn't think too much of Berlin. I didn't enjoy the fact that it was an armed city. I didn't like the fact that it was all falling down from the war; that one was supposed to walk around thinking — aah, the spirit of Berlin lives on; in these hallowed walls we'll destroy another empire. I found it very unarty and unattractive and if drag queens make a city cultured, then Berlin was cultured, because Berlin had Romy Haag and Romy Haag was terrific and her acts were amazing. What they managed to put together in the shape of theatre and art on a very small stage, with limited capabilities in a nightclub, was terrific — absolutely amazing.

"But as I told David — I said 'You can't live here in life from one night to another in a nightclub — I can't do that. There's got to be other things.'

Angie Bowie in 1985. ▼

"From that point we were supposed to have a family Christmas in Switzerland with Zowie but David decided he was going to go to Berlin where he had become involved in filming *Just a Gigolo.*"

It was just prior to Christmas that Angie took a plane to New York leaving Zowie in the care of Marion and Daniella and having spent Christmas with friends in New York, she returned in early January to find the house was empty. Zowie and Marion had been taken to Berlin and the story appeared in the papers a day or two later claiming that David had 'snatched' Zowie because he'd been abandoned.

Having run out of money, and not wanting to call David to ask for any, Angie got in touch with an English journalist in London saying she was ready to give her side of the story, which led to the Sunday Mirror promising to send over cash with the reporter and photographer.

Realizing what she had done, Angie attempted suicide by taking a bottle of sleeping pills and washing them down with a glass of water, a story which subsequently appeared in all the national press followed by a statement issued in Berlin by David Bowie:

"My wife was not aware that my son was with me. A few days before Christmas she decided she would leave Switzerland and spend the holidays with friends elsewhere. From that day to her arrival back on January 2, she didn't phone me or the boy to say where she was."

Angie Bowie: "I leased an apartment from a friend of mine and Leee's on Broadway and 78th Street. Then I tried to kill myself again. I just didn't see a way out at that time. I couldn't see a way of getting divorced, getting my share of the company and life continuing — I just couldn't see it. It was real tricky.

"I met my friends Jan and Steve Bruce again in New York. They were staying at The Waldorf, doing a deal with Long John Baldry with Casablanca and I went to see them and Jan looked at me and she said, 'I think you had better come with us'. I was quite in love with this guy called Keith Paul and I said that I would like to come but I couldn't come right now. I did want to go. I knew that I couldn't stay in New York — there was access to too many things that I wanted when I was depressed.

"About a week later I called Jan and Steve in Los Angeles and I said that I was coming now, tonight. They said OK, there's a first class ticket at the airport. They asked whether I needed a car to get to the airport. I said, 'No, I'm cool'. I went to Los Angeles and they picked me up and then I had a series of like the best year of my life — some of the best adventures I've ever been through, only cluttered up at some stage when Jan and I had to go to Switzerland for legal things to do with the divorce, which didn't happen then because I couldn't get representation in Switzerland. They basically wanted to leave me absolutely potless and David had all the ammunition and evidence that he needed to do that."

The Sun: "Rock superstar David Bowie admitted yesterday that he snatched his 6-year-old son from his wife. He did it, he claimed, because his wife Angie left the boy with only his Nanny for company at Christmas. Bowie ordered the Nanny to bring the child from the couple's Swiss home to West Berlin where he's making a film.

"David and Angie have a free and easy style of marriage. They've admitted that each have lovers of both sexes. At the weekend, 28-year-old Angie said that David had taken Zowie without her knowledge while she was visiting New York, and she wants a divorce to get custody of the boy. At her home in Switzerland she said, 'I have spoken to police here and when you are married, they can't do anything.'

"Bowie is in Berlin making the black comedy film *Just A Gigolo* with Kim Novak, Maria Schnell and David Hemmings."

Daily Mirror: "Drama at Snow Chalet in Switzerland." It was bylined Tony Robinson, Geneva.

"It was a sight I will never forget. There, crumpled at the foot of the stairs lay Angie Bowie. Her face was covered in blood. Angie, wife of pop star David Bowie, had tried to kill herself in a fit of anxiety over her son on Bowie's birthday seven days ago. She swallowed three handfuls of pills and tried to stab herself with a carving knife and finally threw herself down the stairs. Angie, 28, was unconscious on and off for nearly two days and when she recovered in hospital with a broken nose, two black eyes and cuts and bruises, she revealed to me that she had been expecting her lover's child. Later, her pop musician boy friend, Keith Paul, who has been living with Angie in a luxurious rented chalet in Switzerland, told me, 'If I hadn't been there to help her, she would have died.'

"I'd gone to see Angie at the cuckoo-clock chalet on the snow covered slopes of Lake Geneva after she asked for the Sunday Mirror's help in resolving her anxieties over her 6-year-old son. We were able to establish that while she had been on a visit to America, David Bowie had invited young Zowie and the boy's young Nanny to join him in Berlin where he is making a film. Zowie was returned to Angie on the Thursday night. With him was his Nanny, a bodyguard and another woman. Earlier when I spoke to her on the plane, she was furious, almost hysterical and said that she was seeking a divorce so that she could get legal custody of Zowie."

Dana Gillespie: "Angie was supportive, even when the collapse of the marriage went on. I never heard her say to Zowie, 'You know, your father's treating you like a shit'. She always said, 'Daddy is great'. She always helped totally to make him love the father and I always think it's a bit unfair, the end result, because there is no reason for anybody to be enemies on this earth. He must really feel threatened by her that he just doesn't want to make any communication, or he can't forget some of the bad things that went on.

"A lot of bad things went on. I mean, Angie fell to pieces in a way because she lost everything. She always said she wanted to be the only one that never took him for a ride financially. She could have steamed in for a hell of a lot with one of those heavy lawyers, but she didn't. It's very noble of her but probably, in retrospect, might be seen as folly. But even then, he got so much bigger in the 80's, you had no idea how much was at stake. But I think morally she was right not to have been a bitch about it. I don't approve of ex-wives steaming in on their husbands. But she did lose — not just the husband — she lost a kind of a life style and things that she had worked towards for years. It's not a productive thing that you see, like a song or something. He might write something and she would tell him it's great. She would encourage him. She'd never say that it was a piece of shit and he'd throw it in the wastepaper basket. That was one positive side."

In Paris to promote 'Low' and to film video promo for 'Be My Wife'. ▶▶

A NEW CAREER IN A NEW TOWN

F I V E

Attending Paris première of 'The Man Who Fell To Earth' with Sydne Rome (later to be David's co-star in 'Just A Gigolo')

▶

Taken from the original artwork by Bowie for the promotion of 'Ashes To Ashes'. ▶▶

David Bowie's 1976 World Tour opened in Vancouver in February and differed from previous shows by incorporating a black and white film made in 1922 by Salvador Dali and Louis Bunuel called *Un Chien Andalou.* The stage setting was stark monochrome, black stage with white strip lighting, uncluttered and minimal by comparison with previous tours.

Just prior to the tour, manager Michael Lipman was added to the list of discarded managers. He wasn't the only employee to be sacked at this point. Bowie also axed, at the last moment, two of his backing singers, *Ava Cherry* and *Claudia Linear.* The large entourage that had accompanied him on the Diamond Dogs Tour had now disappeared.

During the 1976 World Tour Angie flew over to Switzerland to secure their residency in that country, and then went on to find the Cuckoo-Clock House, the house in which she attempted suicide.

By the end of the 1976 tour, David had moved to West Berlin and work had begun on the album 'Low', which would be released the following January, with Carlos Alomar, Tony Visconti and Brian Eno. The following spring David toured England with Iggy Pop. The tour subsequently moved on to Canada and then the United States, culminating in David's and Iggy's return to Berlin for work on Iggy's next album.

Later that year David appeared on *Marc,* Marc Bolan's television show, singing a live version of his forthcoming single "Heroes", followed by an appearance on Bing Crosby's '*Merry Old Christmas*' TV show during which he performed a duet with Crosby "*The Little Drummer Boy*". The show was to be Bing Crosby's last TV appearance before his death in October and, tragically, Marc Bolan died in a car crash on Barnes Common in West London shortly after the recording. David flew in from Switzerland to attend the funeral.

A family Christmas in Switzerland with Angie and Zowie was planned for 1977 but this was not to be — David decided to spend Christmas in Berlin and Angie left Switzerland to visit friends in New York. It was the Christmas that Zowie was left with his nanny, and David, having flown to Switzerland, took both Zowie and the nanny back to Berlin with him. It was just after Christmas, in the January of 1978, that Angie attempted suicide.

The following month, with the filming of *Just A Gigolo* complete, David flew out of Berlin to Kenya prior to going back to the States for preparation of the 1978 World Tour. This was the most arduous tour David had ever undertaken, with dates in the United States, Europe, the UK, Australia and Japan. This tour incorporated the white neon tube effect that had been developed by lighting engineer Eric Barrett on the 1976 tour. On stage he wore a white sailor's outfit — baggy trousers, shirt and a

snakeskin jacket — and a sailor's hat, an outfit that was designed by Natasha Kornilof.

Natasha Kornilof: "David was filming 'Just a Gigolo' in Berlin when the plans were laid for the 1978 World Tour for which I did a whole wardrobe for him.

"Firstly I had to go to Berlin for a meeting. Oh God! The travel arrangements went wrong. . . so I arrived there late in the evening having sent telex messages ahead hoping that somebody would pick them up on the way. You know, you launch these things into the blue and wonder what's going to happen at the other side.

"Coco met me in Berlin and we drove off to where David was filming *Just A Gigolo*. It was cold – it was freezing. There was black ice all over the place and I barely saw Berlin through the gloom. Coco and I discovered that, at separate times, we had been to the same convent kindergarten in Kashmir which seemed a long shot but we had — quite extraordinary.

"We waited until he had finished filming and then Coco took me to my hotel and I was feeling dreadful. We did some drawings for each other on the back of envelopes which was all we had.

"When I returned, I sat down to a lot of hard work based on these scribbles that we had done on the back of envelopes and torn bits of magazine, and started the basis of a wardrobe. Although David had made a brief visit to London during this time, I didn't see him but I sent some of the stuff over to him where he tried it on and sent it back with messages like 'more of this — one in red as well please'.

"So I just got on with it until eventually I was to fly to Dallas where they were rehearsing with all this stuff."

Sean Mayes: "We were rehearsing in Dallas for the World Tour and got the whole two hour show together in just two weeks, which seemed impossible. I went out there in fear and trembling because I had come from a rock and roll band and I thought I'm going to be facing all these top line musicians and am going to be way out of my depth but it wasn't like that. It seemed very easy in a way. Carlos would give us a list of chords if we needed them and all the musicians were very friendly. We were all different but all got on well.

"We were staying in a horrible hotel outside Dallas and rehearsing in a big warehouse just down the road from the hotel because that's where the equipment company was based for the tour. That's why we were in Dallas, because I was thinking 'Why on earth Dallas?' We rehearsed for about three days before David arrived. Outside was blazing sunshine and inside the place was fairly dark and then the door opened at the end of the room and the sun blazed in and three people came in and one of them was a very tanned, thin and brown — David had just flown in from Africa.

"The rehearsals were strange because Carlos was in charge and all the time David seemed very much to be behaving like a kid, as if he was his own kid brother who got the chance to jump up and sing with the band sometimes. He'd forget the words and apologise and look silly and laugh and it was all very easy like that. What was nice, for me anyway, about the 78 Tour — for all of us as musicians — was David had picked us all out for various different odd reasons but basically he picked us because he liked the way we played and given that, he then wasn't going to try and make us play in some different way."

Natasha Kornilof: "I arrived at Dallas airport with

Back on the road in '78. ▶

two huge suitcases full of David's wardrobe and a little one which was full of mine.

"That night, I was so high on tiredness that I couldn't sleep. I didn't know what time it was — I think it was dawn for me. But anyway, we all went to a French restaurant in Dallas. Have you ever heard of such madness? They eat frogs' legs or something and I can't eat frogs. I thought 'I'm in Dallas and I'll have steak', which was very good, but everyone else was sick.

"When I got back to the hotel, I tried to put myself to sleep which seemed impossible and I leapt up at something like six in the morning and grabbed the telephone and said 'I must have an iron. I must have an electric iron. I've got all these clothes I've got to iron'. I was thinking to myself that I must iron these clothes before David sees them because they're a terrible mess. I'd unpacked them and hung them up by now. The hotel was quite nice with me. As Texans they had to deal with this mad European lady shrieking around. They said they might manage an iron around 10 o'clock in the morning but it would be better if I went back to sleep.

"We didn't have a 'try-on' of the clothes until about lunch time that day. I think it was Easter Sunday or Good Friday — it was over Easter anyway — and it was very extraordinary, nothing really was happening. Anyway, we had a 'try-on' of the clothes and made some decisions. There was a rather large variety and I'd already made decisions about them and then David made alternative decisions and we mixed different things together until we arrived at something we thought would work."

Sean Mayes: "The funniest story — Tony Mascia, David's big minder, was in the hotel and Natasha had asked for a sewing machine to be delivered to the hotel on hire so she could run over some of the clothes and do alterations, and this guy came along to deliver it and Natasha wasn't around, and this guy was trying to demonstrate to Tony Mascia how to use this sewing machine. Tony was saying that this didn't mean anything to him but this guy just kept on trying to show him, so eventually Tony just picked him up gently put him outside the door and closed the door."

Natasha Kornilof: "We spent another couple of days in Dallas and then we flew to San Diego. I must admit I was glad to leave Dallas. I was not keen on it at all. Neither was John Kennedy, I suppose, but there you go.

"We flew to San Diego which was different. I just sat in this hotel room, which had a little balcony, and finished off my endless sewing. There was enough work to keep me occupied without driving me mad. It was really very pleasant indeed.

"Then came the great opening which was wonderful. I'd never been to one of these, let alone been back stage. It was really very glamorous to me because most of my profession is unglamorous. People think it's a glamorous profession. They say 'You must meet all the stars'. Rubbish! The most fascinating people I meet are haberdashers. But this was wonderful. This huge stadium with masses of security men back stage. And amazing cars. David's car was quite amazing because it was the one he had in *The Man Who Fell To Earth.* A beautiful thing. You could have a little soirée in the back because it seated several people very comfortably with a table in between.

"A nice San Diego catering lady had come along and put this Japanese meal out which no-one ate. I was starving and dying to eat this but it was full of raw fish and nobody could take the chance of eating it, but it was all beautifully laid out with cubes of ice keeping the raw fish happy.

"David is a funny eater. He occasionally pecks and then he suddenly eats something very extraordinary at the worst time of day or night and then he'll peck again. And he pecked before the show I can tell you.

"There was this dressing room and we had all the costumes hung on the rails around him. It's basically what he wanted to do. He would stride in and decide what he was going to wear that night. He did a change of costume in San Diego and I saw the whole show with the catering lady (we became very good friends and stood at the side and watched it). It was magic. I'd never been to one of these huge rock concerts back stage although I'd been to them out front because I'd seen some of David's concerts when he did 'Young Americans' in London, and having done some odds and ends there that they needed at the last minute, I got a ticket. Being out front it was amazing but backstage was even more wonderful — quite magic."

Sean Mayes: "The stage setting was a development of the 1976 Tour when David used all that neon light. On this tour we had a complete backdrop of neon tubes 16 foot high and God knows how wide, and more neon I think above us. We were really, effectively, playing in a box of white light surrounded on three sides and above, and below the floor was black, shiny flexiglass, so it was all reflected back, and I had a couple of film floods behind me and I was playing in sort of funky plastic jacket which literally melted during the course of the tour because the lights were so hot.

"There weren't any very special effects. The lighting was very effective and yet simple. It was all this white light but then again yellow white light, harsh white light and neon light — all the different whites. We all wore whatever we liked which was very varied stuff. I was, as I say, a sort of coffee table punk. Carlos started in rather svelte velvet clothes and ended up looking almost as punk as I did. Different people wore different things and David had all the clothes that Natasha did. I don't even know that he suggested any ideas. I think he said 'I would like a snake skin drape coat' or something and she made that, but most of it was just some of these, some of those and what-have-you, and came up with them all.

"It wasn't a staged show but everyone moved like a band and David just had a good time and enjoyed himself and smiled a lot. He seemed to be very much enjoying on stage. Whether he was being himself or not, he was certainly playing David Bowie as opposed to playing someone else and it made it very enjoyable to do.

"This was San Diego. You open the tour generally at a place not too big and famous, so we had about three or four gigs before the first 'biggy' which was Los Angeles but nonetheless, it was big — it was 15,000 people in a big stadium. We were all very keyed up for it. We had finished rehearsals in Dallas about a week before, so we hadn't had any rehearsals until then, David's voice was not in absolute tip-top shape, so we couldn't do too much for the run-through before the show and we were all terrified of making bad mistakes. We were back stage and we all walked out behind the stage ready to go on, waiting for the word from Eric, the tour manager, and we were all feeling very, very nervous and I just started jumping up and down to warm up and get rid of the nerves and then we all started doing this pogo-ing which helped the nerves a lot. Then Eric said, 'Let's go', and we literally walked round the edge of the stage — the stage was raised obviously — there weren't curtains and things because we were at one end of an indoor sports stadium — so we walked out and the house lights were still on. We just walked round and up the steps and onto the stage and first of all people obviously didn't realize it was beginning. They'd been waiting for the lights to go down and all that and then gradually they realized and started to make a noise and this noise gradually spread through the whole crowd.

"The first number was 'Warszawa' which is a slow six minute instrumental. It starts as a synthesizer thing at the front of the stage. Carlos was right at the front as a conductor with a baton with his back to the crowd and literally conducting us all in (it was a very slow number so you had to have someone conducting) and with each boom the stage light would just show their first glow and the house lights go down a fraction, and the next boom they'd go down further, and with each boom there'd be this thrill from the crowd until eventually after several bars the place was dark and the stage was bright and the lights got brighter and brighter so your eyes were streaming. It was a very slow, controlled number but at the end of it, a couple of beats from the drums and straight into 'Heroes' and the whole place erupted — wow, this is it, the show is really beginning. The nerves somehow got us through it all and we didn't make any dreadful mistakes."

Carlos Alomar: "My relationship with David is that of band leader and artist. When David turns round and looks at the band he only looks at me. I give him cues and he gives me cues. I'm dancing and singing — he's dancing and singing. The thing is the band has got to be in the best spirits always which is one of the reasons that David and I have been working together so well. He gives me the band and I take care of them, spiritually, mentally, anything they need. I make sure they're nice and comfortable.

"So, the band usually has to look at me and they get their cues from me. If David gives them a cue they don't take a cue from David, they take the cue from me. If David cues me and I don't cue the band, then the band doesn't hit and then David will look at me and say 'Carlos, what are you doing?' But the band doesn't usually have to take any fall and it's been this way for a long time. It started after the 'Diamond Dogs' tour after he finished with *Mike Garson* and *Dave Sandbourn* and the other musicians who were with him on that album.

London première ticket, the event attended by Bowie. ▼

Actually it works out better for us because the rhythm section that he used at that time was myself, Dennis Davis and George Murray, and he kept that rhythm section for the longest time whereas in the past he'd never really kept any musicians, but they were kept for three or four albums or two or three tours.

"As people, no matter what happens, we always come back to the same thing, no matter what the business people are doing. I depend on him and he depends on me. It's really fortunate. It's not going to last forever — or I certainly don't think so — but during the time that it's happening, it's pretty much fun.

"There was a time when David used to say, 'Look, I'm going to change the music, I'm going to change the song. The way I'm going to do it is by getting rid of Carlos'. It was in the papers and everything, but then a tour came up and he couldn't do it in the time that he'd given himself, so he called me back to do it. I can understand that if that comfort is going to. . . You see, that's the one thing it is — comfort — so when he feels strong enough to just go out there by himself without me, then it will all be over."

Natasha Kornilof: "At the end of the show David goes off stage while they're still playing and he's smuggled off. The rest of you get locked in for about an hour and a half before it's deemed clear to let the rest of the entourage go. Then comes a really frightening thing. You're put in these cars and told on no account to open any windows or doors. To lock all doors and see that they're firmly locked. We were in David's car and Tony was driving. These huge doors went up at the back of the stadium — enormous steel rollers — and the crowd swarmed in and banged on the cars. They just had to keep driving through this — it was horrifying. I had not expected it and it was quite a terrifying experience. I think we'd have been torn apart if they'd managed to get in. I thought to myself, 'Imagine experiencing this night after night wherever you go.' It must have a very strange effect on one and I was glad it was not actually directed at me I can tell you.

"We went back to the hotel where there's always someone who finds out which floor the group are on, so you've got to run through loads of fans."

Sean Mayes: "After kicking off in San Diego, the tour did three months in America and Canada and then went over to Europe and from Europe on to Britain — Glasgow, Edinburgh, the Midlands and London. Then we had two months break and during that time we cut 'Lodger' in Switzerland, and then it was off to Australia, New Zealand and Japan.

"It was odd recording 'Lodger'. There was this great big studio on the lake in Switzerland and also a small studio in the same complex. David chose to use the little studio which was rather small. It was the third album that he was doing with Brian Eno and he and Brian were determining the direction that everything would take. Basically we were getting down backing tracks. In some cases he knew what the song was about and what the words were going to be, but with plenty of them he was just putting together sounds and backing tracks and didn't write any words until after the tour was over.

"All the songs would have working titles which sometimes would be completely abandoned and we were using funny ways to put the music together. We'd be given say a chord sequence and a rhythm and in one case, in fact, we had a chart of chords up on the wall and Brian would just point to different chords with a baton and when he wanted to do a different chord, we'd change and play that one. It

was a very odd way of doing things and it seemed deliberately to make things difficult for us. In other words, if anyone was getting too comfortable with what they were playing, he'd then change it and give them something else, so you were making mistakes all the time. But you'd play the same thing over and over and it would all be recorded and then at the end of the day he and Tony Visconti would run off just an ordinary quarter inch tape that they'd then take away and listen to it and chop it up — literally chop it up with scissors and put it together again.

"Apparently, what he was doing, as often as not, was picking the section with the most mistakes in — perhaps that would be the verse — and that would be looped to make two verses and then looped again to make a couple of verses later on. Because the mistakes come up again each time, they cease to be mistakes — they become part of the music. The looping they'd done on the quarter inch tape would be duplicated on the multi-track which would then be copied again on to another multi-track, so that you'd end up with the structure of a song in multi-track made from the loops and so on that you could continue adding to, so that as you continue to layer on top of that, it ceased to be obvious that it came from loops in the first place. Very odd way of working."

Brian Eno: "I'd often be treating things while the musicians were playing. I was trying to make some kind of sonic character to the track so that the thing had a distinct textural feeling that gave it a mood to begin with. There'd be quite a lot of that going on. It's hard to describe because it was never the same twice. It's not susceptible to description very easily in ordinary musical terms. It would just be doing the thing that you can do with tape which is you can treat the music as malleable. You have something down there you can start squeezing it around and changing the colour of this and putting this thing much further in front of something else, and so on. It would be stage two and quite a lot of that would be going on.

"The third album, 'Lodger', did not have such a celebratory feel to it. I thought it was a more miserable situation — less excitement, less conviction, more a feeling of, 'Well, time to do a record I guess'. 'Product commitment phase' they call that I think, although that might be a harsh judgement. It wasn't a conscious move towards marketing I don't think, it was more a case of, 'Well look, we've got to get a record done — let's not have too much pissing about this time'. For me the pissing about was the interesting bit. I don't say that the record was without experimentation or without its good points, but for me as a recording experience, it was not so interesting. I'd been through things like that before. I suppose also at the time I was losing interest in the whole business anyway and I thought this music cannot be a container for the things I'm interested in any more, so I have to invent a new kind of music.

"I suppose I was marking time a little bit on that record, waiting to see whether anything would come up that would change my mind. I'd be very happy to have my mind changed you know. There are sorts of quite mercenary reasons for wanting to be in that market but in fact I'd got nothing to say in the market any more — I think. I had my suspicions. I'd released 'Music For Airports' then which I was very very pleased with. I was pleased with it after the event as well. When you release records, you experience quite different emotions about them — quite unexpected ones once they've hit the market.

"I always think that a piece of music isn't finished

96

until it's released because when it's released, you suddenly hear it through all those other ears — all those ears who haven't had all your excuses and defences of the record, who just stick to it like any other record. And what do they hear? They hear this. When that happens you think, 'What are they hearing?' What does it mean to somebody for whom there is no history, for whom there is no result to a chain of aesthetic decisions that have a kind of logic to them, but just an isolated incident in the world of music for them.

"I was feeling more and more that rock music was just adding to the heap and that's what I think it is largely now. I think it's a dead bore quite honestly, but it will continue for years like big band jazz continues. It's not a form where anyone expects anything exciting to come out of but it's still on Radio 2 all the time — well Radio 1 is Radio 2 of tomorrow.

"When I released 'Music For Airports', I thought I'd put something into the world. I thought I'd made a musical space that didn't exist before and I still do. The reactions I get about that indicate that some other people do as well and that's what interests me. I'm interested in making new spaces and for a while I think I did that in rock music but then I thought I wasn't doing it any more, so now I do it somewhere else.

"For a start, I don't owe anything to anybody. I'm not in 'product commitment phase' — never have been and never will be. Secondly, I pay for all my own work myself so I'm never in a position of feeling that I've disappointed somebody who has invested money in me. I pay for it myself and then I offer it to someone and if they don't like it, I'll offer it to someone else. As it happens, my records sell. Not badly. They don't sell millions but they sell OK. They sell with almost no need for assistance from the record company so it's actually not such a bad deal for them. They put these things on the market and I'm sure they think 'God knows why people should buy them, but why should we complain.' We don't have to have big ad campaigns because I tell them not to anyway. They don't have to service the thing in anyway. They don't have to service expensive tours. It's a kind of pot-boiler for the record companies. They're quite kind to me and also I think they imagine there is the possibility of me bringing in some big act like Elvis."

Sean Mayes: "On the 'Lodger' session, they were using this pack of cards that was developed by Brian Eno and a friend called 'Oblique Strategies'. You'd basically just take random cards from the pack that would say things like 'start again' or 'new idea round the corner' which are instructions that are fairly random and at times fairly difficult to understand but you've got to take what it means to you at the time. I can't remember the particular things but it was put together as a pack of cards and you would then just shuffle the cards and cut them and pick one out. Whenever you had a problem or you weren't sure what to do, you'd then cut the pack and take a card and decide on the basis of that. This was also a very odd way of working.

"Obviously a lot of stuff was done that was thrown out later and yet, despite that, the whole thing was put together very fast indeed. It wasn't a matter of saying, 'We haven't got a good take here, let's go for another one'. You just do it — play for 15 minutes or so and then move on and do something else. I was there for five days and I actually worked for two and a half of those days — that was getting the basic tracks down. Then there came an afternoon when David and I worked and we put down the solo on 'Fantastic Voyage' and on one of the others. Tony Visconti was down in the control room and David would nip up and down between the control room and the piano. It all seemed extraordinarily casual.

"In one of the things I had to play three times, note for note, which I thought was beyond me but I did actually manage to do it in the stress of the moment, and they had the tape playing at very slightly different speeds each time so that when the three were all put together, it gave it an underwater wobble sound. This was during the course of the afternoon — we whipped through all the tracks doing a bit here and a bit there and I had to concentrate very hard while I was doing it.

"At the end of the time I was left with practically no memory of anything I'd done, a bit as if you'd spent an afternoon phoning people up and at the end of the day you can't remember any of the phone numbers. It was a bit like that and very odd.

"Coco travelled everywhere with David on the tour. She was his sort of personal assistant, minder, personal manager, wet nurse, companion, whatever. She would sort out anything that needed to be sorted out. She's a strange person in as much as she really has no life of her own. It's an odd thing. What she does is probably what a lot of fans think they'd love to do and would probably stick it for about three months and go off their heads. I got on very well with her — fortunately — because in a way, it was more important to get on with Corinne than to get on with David, but fortunately I got on with both of them like a house on fire.

"There was a certain amount of friction between Coco and *Pat Gibbons,* who was David's manager at the time. I suppose they were both managing David in their different ways and in different areas and some of the areas would overlap and so on. Coco would look after his clothes on tour and pack his bags and all that sort of thing. Obviously she must

◄

Sporting Natasha's costume (complete with fake snake-skin jacket).

The '78 shuffle. ▲

have done other things I suppose — if he wanted to make notes or get in touch with someone or whatever, she'd probably do all that for him — personal assistant simply. She was there; she was part of the set up. She made David's life much easier.

"On that tour David was very relaxed and looking very healthy. When we started the Australian part of the tour, somebody had lent us a boat and we were all out in this boat in the sun, all in our swim suits and things, and David was pulling at his middle and just about managing to pinch a bit of flesh between his fingers and saying, 'Dear me, they'll be calling me plump next.' Back in 1973 for instance, he must have been doing drugs then — his skin had this translucent look because he had his bright red hair then, as if all the blood had left his body and gone up into his hair — he looked very strange indeed. But he looked very solid and healthy on the 78 Tour."

Carlos Alomar: "David did suffer somewhat because he had five years off after the White Light Tour. Five years off is a long time for anybody to break. During that time there was a real reluctance to do it, but it had to be done. He was going through problems with Angie — he wanted to have his kid — and I'd just had a kid so I wanted to get off the road too. So we decided to go off the road. Little did we know that it would be for five years.

"He started changing during that period because then you're going through the self realization that you want to do something else. It's not so easy to do something else — you want to do movies, you've done a few movies and now you're typecast. Now what do you do? Any field you enter, you always get to that place where you have to look around and say, 'What the hell am I doing here? Now that I'm here, where am I?' It happened after that White Light tour. That's when he was on his own. He wanted to just concentrate on the movies and

suddenly he wasn't getting the movies. He wasn't getting the album support. He wasn't getting the record deal. Nothing was happening."

Natasha Kornilof: "It wasn't long after the 1978 World Tour that I was to do the Blue Clown costume for 'Scary Monsters And Super Creeps'. That was the next big thing and it was lovely to do — I really enjoyed it. David rang me up from somewhere foreign. He always rings up and says, 'Tash', (he always sounds the same). I said, 'What do you want?' to which he replied, 'You know the beautiful clown in the circus?' 'Yes, I know' I said. 'Well, I want to be the most beautiful.' 'All right', I told him. 'Do you think blue?' He agreed. So I went away and did it. He didn't actually see it until it was complete but he pointed out that he wanted a high neck. Of course, Lindsay Kemp always said that with those costumes you must have a low neck because the neck is very important for clowning and

On tour in 1978.

doing any sort of mime. With the high neck he looked like a Jacobean prince — it was almost too much — so I had to go away and cut the neck down and put the collar back on a low neck and then it really looked like a clown. I ran up a little hat and off we went to the photo session for the cover of the album.

"It was quite an epic for me and unfortunately, there isn't a drawing of it because I threw it away afterwards as I didn't think it was going to be used on every poster everywhere. Although I keep loads of paper around the house, I've never found the drawing I did for that costume. It just disappeared. I think we must have used it for wiping down the table or something and I could kick myself now. At the time, it was just another clown costume. I'd done the drawing and I'd basically used fabrics that were in the house — that's how I design best — and I never throw anything away. It's my treasure."

Tony Visconti: " 'Scary Monsters And Super Creeps' was the first real attempt at making a truly

commercial album and to stop the experimenting, so we hired Power Station Studios in New York, which is probably the most glossy studio in New York and was famous at the time for the Bruce Springsteen drum sound because they had this great cavernous room made out of wood with two microphones stuffed way up high in the ceiling which could be lowered on a mechanism, and as we wanted to go for that big ambient drum sound it was ideal, and it was a sound we achieved.

"We did about two and a half weeks of furious recording and David was the most prepared for that album as he'd ever been. A few of the songs were actually completed before which was rare, because David usually writes on the spot. Things like 'Ashes To Ashes' were conceived as chord changes — there was no melody — and it was actually called 'People Are Turning To Gold', but nevertheless, the approach to that album was very professional and very slick and we were going for our first real slick sound in years. It was shortly after this that he was approached by *Jack Hofsiss* to play John Merrick in *The Elephant Man.*"

The Sun: "Rock star David Bowie wowed Broadway yesterday with a brilliant performance in one of the theatre's toughest roles. He won rave reviews and a standing ovation on the opening night of *The Elephant Man*. Earlier New York critics had slammed the choice of Bowie to play the deformed 19th century cripple as a gimmick but last night they described him as shockingly good, splendid and very moving. Bowie plays John Merrick, a man who was exhibited in circus shows in Victorian times.

"David Bowie's single 'Ashes to Ashes' was a No. 1 success and his album 'Scary Monsters' is also shooting up the charts. David has always been unpredictable to say the least and just as he is receiving all sorts of praise and attention once again from the music industry, he now sets his sights on a new career, stage acting. He has recently been playing the part of *The Elephant Man,* a strangely deformed 19th century character to much critical acclaim in the United States."

Jack Hofsiss: "His appropriateness for the part, as far as I could tell having seen his work up to that point, was a combination of both his film work, which was more traditional work, and his concert work on stage. The latter proved to me — more than just showed me — that he could obviously take care of himself on the stage and he was born to that sort of work. In the roles that he played in films, he had a strong affinity for the part because of the isolation of a lot of the characters he'd played. (*The Man Who Fell To Earth* most prominently I would say).

"We got together socially and chatted about the play. That started the seed to grow in my mind and I planted it in his very casually because I knew that I would be asking him to give up a large period of time but at the same time didn't want to shock him and say, 'Come and do this thing every night for the next nine months' as that can be fairly shocking to someone who hadn't done that, which is a necessary discipline in the theatre.

"Eventually we sat down and had a conversation and talked a bit about the character. Strangely enough, the play is set in the same section of London that David grew up in, so he tells me, which was an interesting connection and a strong bond between himself and the role. From there we took off to our mutual satisfaction and did the business work and then started.

"I tried to paint as black a picture of how it would be (doing the same thing every night for nine months) as I could. I told him that he would have a lot of freedom but he couldn't arrange scenes like he rearranges numbers in a rock concert, as the other people would be terribly confused if he tried to do that. So he took it on as a challenge although I think it was a running joke throughout the whole experience, the fact that it was going to be exactly the same tonight as it was last night, no matter what one does.

"There is one secret to playing that character I always find, which is not for the actor playing it to ever find the character sad. His particular way of doing it was to give the guy a worthiness, a street-wise quality which would have come from growing up in one of the tougher neighbourhoods in town as both of them did, so that made it very interesting. The other actors who had played the role successfully had given the man a more neo-classical austerity but David had a 'you've got to tell me that twice before I'm going to believe you' feeling which gave the character humour and a vitality that was essential to a successful portrayal of the man and, I think, the

THE BOOTH THEATRE
Gerald Schoenfeld, *Chairman* ⑤ A Shubert Organization Theatre
RICHMOND CRINKLEY   Bernard B. Jacobs, *President*
ELIZABETH I. McCANN
PRESENT   NELLE NUGENT

DAVID BOWIE
DONAL DONNELLY   PATRICIA ELLIOTT
IN THE AMERICAN NATIONAL THEATRE AND ACADEMY PRODUCTION OF
THE ELEPHANT MAN
BY BERNARD POMERANCE
RICHARD CLARKE   JEFFREY JONES   JUDITH BARCROFT   DENNIS CREAGHAN
AND I.M. HOBSON
CELLIST: MICHAEL GOLDSCHLAGER
SETTING BY DAVID JENKINS   COSTUMES BY JULIE WEISS   LIGHTING BY BEVERLY EMMONS
ASSOCIATE PRODUCERS RAY LARSEN and TED SNOWDON
PRODUCTION SUPERVISOR: BRENT PEEK
DIRECTED BY JACK HOFSISS
The Producers and Theatre Management are Members of The League of New York Theatres and Producers, Inc.

Hot footing from the Booth ▲
Theatre, Broadway.

◄

Taking his bows in 'The Elephant Man'

kernel for his success in the role.

"I think he found it thrilling to be on Broadway and I also think he felt privileged to tell this man's story as we did. Broadway is exciting but it is still the same little room that you sit in every night waiting for your entrance, and they're not very glamorous on Broadway. No matter how many flowers you stuff into them, they are still these little cubicles where you sit hot and tired. It's a very demanding role physically, even though the excitement is there, and the array of people that came to see him was a particular joy for us all.

"He had to prove himself with the theatre people. Theatre people are a tough crowd, particularly about people in the rock world. Theatre people pride themselves in their discipline and rock people seem, by reputation alone, if not in reality, to be undisciplined to say the least. That wasn't the case with David Bowie although he still had to prove himself. Virtually every one of the actors in the cast took me aside at one point and asked me whether I thought it was a wise idea, to which I replied 'I hope so', although I could have been proved wrong. David was very earnest and serious about knowing all his words, much more so than the other actors ironically, who were sloppy.

"David first went out to Denver to play the show. We had a national company touring the States at the time and I didn't feel it was wise (and he didn't want to) to walk onto a Broadway stage for the first time in front of everybody, so off we went to Denver. The theatre there was about 1200 seats and downstairs was a sea of grey headed people who had bought their tickets in advance and upstairs there were seats that were sold particularly for that performance, which were filled with young people. When he came out on stage, there was huge applause from upstairs and at the end of the show, when he came for his curtain call, there was a standing ovation and it was begun by the people downstairs. I thought it was a great compliment to everybody. It was truly wonderful.

"David had an uncanny sensitivity to the man's life experience, an ability to project that into a theatrical piece and to understand the inherent story-telling nature of a dramatic event like a play. I can happily say he is a good actor. He loves an audience , which I think is extremely important, and has great respect for the collaboration with other actors which is essential. You must both act and react. It's very easy with that role, because the character lives so isolated from other people, not to relate with the other actors on the stage, but luckily that wasn't a problem and proved to be another key to his success I think.

"I found him to be a very serious individual and that proved to be the case both socially and in a work situation. Actually, I tend to be a little more jokey when I work so, in a way, I should straighten up because we were doing this very serious play, but I find that you have to fool around a bit and the other people who have worked exclusively in the theatre did too. So, one of the big things was to try and break him up because he was so earnest about it all which was great. I hope that we did it in a gentle way and in a supportive way and not in a provocative way, but he certainly rose to the occasion in any case."

Julie Weiss (Make-up artist with *The Elephant Man*): "One of the differences with working with someone like David was that there was a great gift in watching the types of audience. There was, as Jack said, a younger audience and an older audience.

There was quite a democratic cross-section and one of the first times that David performed on Broadway, we were there quite early as the audience came in, and it was just about time for the curtain to go up and Jack had to go down to the front row and ask a gentleman to turn the lights out in his jacket because he had quite an extraordinary garment on with pin lights which would have exceeded the stage into the front row where the gentleman was sitting. It was really quite wonderful to see such a cross-section of people."

Jack Hofsiss: "There was always an interesting array of hair colours in the third row as I recall. There were blue, there were orange — the fact that it was on a 78-year-old lady or a 20-year-old girl didn't really matter. The cast was very aware of the fact that the audiences were really expanded for the play. The play had been running for a while and it was a wonderful serious play which brings a certain kind of audience to the theatre, but David's presence in it made that audience widen and people would come to see a serious play on Broadway for the first time which was remarkable and quite nice.

"There was some standoffishness or shyness with the rest of the cast but that was slightly reinforced by the character because of the nature of the character. The actors would take the relationship that they had with the character on stage and slightly extend it to the off-stage relationship which is done to help one's ability to pop into one's performance at 8 o'clock every night.

"We had to sneak David out of the theatre through various tunnels during the course of the run so, unfortunately, he wasn't able to sit around with the cast afterwards and have a drink and unwind.

"I think he should do more plays although I haven't quite decided what yet, but we do have this conversation every time we see each other. I think he should do a new play, not an old chestnut but a new play. I'd actually like to see him try a Noel Coward comedy. I thought that *Design For Living* might be fun to do because of his elegance and his wit too, which is obviously necessary and very apparent, and is something that is much in demand these days. Style and wit are great to have.

"It was during the course of David playing the role on Broadway that the tragic death of John Lennon occurred and I remember we asked David if he wanted to miss performances but he insisted not, because it was very important for all aspects of the experience to keep playing the role and to appear. It must have been very frightening for him."

Tony Visconti: "I spent an evening with David after seeing The Elephant Man on Broadway and I thought it was great. I felt that that was his real medium although I never really cared for him in films, but on stage he was magnificent. He was really charismatic as he is on his musical gigs and I was really spellbound.

"It was shortly after this he told me all about the rehearsals he was involved in in London and his involvement with Dominic Muldowney and Louis Marks making the production of the Bertholt Brecht play *Baal* and I remember he wanted to record it as a souvenir and said that it was not going to be any big deal and probably wouldn't sell, but felt it should be recorded for posterity. We had long meetings with Dominic which was the first time that I had ever worked with a serious composer and I remember going to see Dominic at the South Bank Complex and going round many winding rooms and hearing the operatic rehearsals and was very impressed.

"On the television programme, the music was

◄

Drawings from the programme.

very simply scored for a few instruments and banjo, but we wanted to record it actually in Berlin in the style of Bertholt Brecht using a typical German pit band or in other words, a small orchestra comprising of one of each instrument — one violin, one viola, one trumpet, one accordion — and that was the way we approached it."

Louis Marks (Producer *Baal* for BBC TV): "The play is the first play that was written by the German dramatist, Bertholt Brecht who also wrote *Threepenny Opera* and *Mother Courage* and various other things. It was written just shortly before the First World War, about 1912 if I'm not mistaken, and it basically tells the story of a character called Baal, who is a poet and singer and a totally amoral person who doesn't want to conform to anything that is happening in the world of his time. What is happening in the world around him is the world of the old Germany, of the forests and the hills and nature of the old values being rapidly overturned by the coming of the 20th century and the concrete jungles. Forests are being chopped down. He foretells of all the things like acid rain and the whole environment being destroyed.

"As a poet and totally uncontrollable and dynamic and creative person, he is simply a rebel against all of that, but he is also a rebel against any kind of morality so that he behaves without any moral compunction towards his girlfriends and his own friends. He is totally without scruple. All that interests him is his own talent and his art. That's the character of Baal and the play is a fairly episodic play that shows in his life.

"The opening scene is at a party held for him by a prominent industrialist who sees himself as a great patron of the arts — a very elegant part with beautiful women and black ties and wonderful food. Baal comes in and just simply walks off with his wife. Basically it's as simple as that. He turns his back on the fellow and doesn't want to know anything about the kind of thing he's offering — he just pulls his wife.

"He has another girlfriend whom he makes pregnant and ditches. He simply goes through life like that. He is the quintessential, amoral artist.

"The play is a succession of scenes interspersed with songs. There is the famous 'Hymn of Baal' which punctuates all the scenes and he performs in

Keith Richards and Bowie flanking Tina Turner. ▼

the play as a poet, a sort of troubadour singer. The character is a singer — an entertainer — so some of the scenes are set in bars where he is actually performing. At one point, he gets a job in a rather seedy nightclub where he performs a semi-pornographic floor show for the rich bourgeois patrons and finally gets himself sacked because he goes a bit too far in the show and insults the patrons. Then he takes himself off to the forest and commits a murder and is eventually caught by the police. He runs away and dies in a camp of lumberjacks in the forest. The starting point was the forest and nature and so on, and he finally goes back there to die.

"It's a curious kind of anarchic play with wonderful music, some of which is written by Brecht himself, some of which was written by Kurt Weill and some of which is just traditional music, so the play called for a character to play Baal who had to combine many things. He had to be able to act, he had to be able to sing in that particular kind of way as a troubadour singer who could perform ballads in the style that you could sing with a banjo (it's required to be a banjo rather than a guitar), and most important of all, in whom one can believe all the things they say in the play about this character of Baal, which is that he has this wonderful talent and that women fall about for him, that he has this ability to go through life destroying his friends and destroying women and yet still be a charismatic figure that people look up to as a kind of hero.

"In looking around for who might play such a part — it wasn't an acting part — it wasn't a part where you could simply go to an actor who could sing. You had to go to a performer because that's what it required. When thinking of how the play would come across it had to work in something like the same way in which it works within the play. In other words, an audience or viewer switching on to this would have to recognize whoever it was playing that part and know he was already a slightly larger than life character.

"We had various thoughts. We didn't know that Bowie could act at all. We had no knowledge of his acting abilities because up to this point, apart from *The Man Who Fell To Earth*, he hadn't done very much acting and it's very difficult to tell from film acting what the talent is (film acting is very different from stage acting) but he had, a few months before this, come into the production of *The Elephant Man* in New York, so we were able to get a tape of him in that production and it was perfectly clear from that that he was an accomplished actor.

"On the basis of that we contacted him and asked him how he felt about the Brecht play. He was very nervous about it at first and asked to see some of the work of the director, Alan Clark, and we sent him over some tapes of Alan's work. The response to that came back within a couple of days very positively. Yes, he was interested. Could we come and meet him. So Alan and I flew off to Switzerland where he lives. We didn't meet him at his house — we met him at an hotel and talked the whole project through. We discussed all aspects of it — not simply the play itself, but how it would work for him coming into a totally new medium, something he hasn't really worked in before, the whole working structure of the production. It was an extremely amicable meeting and then it was up to the lawyers to make the contract. Within three weeks of that, he was on a plane flying over to start work on the production.

"It was the basic BBC fee. He wasn't paid any special high fees or what you might call a 'star fee'. He worked for the same kind of money that any

▲
French promotion for 'The Hunger'.

actor working at the BBC would be paid. In other words he did it because he wanted to do it. He was fascinated by the play and the work and was looking, at that stage, to enlarge his whole area of work. In fact, I remember him saying in that meeting in Switzerland that there was a limit to how long he could go on doing tours. There comes a point when you actually have to quit. Alongside of that, he had one more tour to do at that point, he wanted to embark on a career of acting. In fact, he's done it — he's made two or three films since then.

"As an artist, he's very interested in art and paints a great deal. He's very much into the early 20th century German art — expressionist art — so he knew the background to the play extremely well and he knew the Brecht song and had, in fact, already recorded separately some of these Brecht songs in a separate context.

"The whole project came at the right time for him and he came at the right time for us so it was a sort of lucky marrying — a luck chance that it all fitted together. That's why it wasn't the straight commercial offer. 'Would you like to play the part? The fee is this'. The thing intrigued him and the fee was never going to be a major factor that was going to stop him doing it.

"At the time he had to have a bodyguard because it was shortly after the Lennon shooting that he came over to rehearse and he was insistent that no-one should know he was here and that the whole thing should be totally under wraps, that the studio should be sealed. There was no question of any fans being involved and also, he would do no interviews while he was here. We abided by this, so much so that I never knew where he was staying. I had to contact him through RCA records I think it was. I was given a contact number where I could talk to his

Publicity, '83 style. ▼

lady manager Coco. I could only contact Coco and she would pass the messages.

"It was a slightly ludicrous situation because if I wanted to talk to him any time between 10.00 in the morning and 5.30 in the evening I'd just roll along to the rehearsal room and we'd have a chat and solve the problem. Any other time I had to go through this elaborate ritual of ringing and leaving messages all because of this slightly exaggerated sense of personal security that he had.

"I suppose it was partly understandable because of the Lennon killing, and I think that all internationally famous rock stars were feeling very nervous at this point so it was explicable, but there was this wonderful contrast between the artificial way one had to deal with him because of the security and then the total informality and friendliness and relaxed atmosphere of the actual work. Once you were in the rehearsal room and chatting to him it was a totally different situation. We would discuss problems and it was all extremely painless I think.

"The worst problems we had, which were nothing to do with Bowie, but endemic with the BBC was the noise from a drill. It was a very heavy schedule as Baal was in every single scene so he was on the studio set for the entire five days, four days of which were the acting scenes in which he also had to sing and the fifth day was for recording of the separate songs because the link songs — the 'Hymn Of Baal' and the various songs which linked the scenes — were being sung full close-up, straight into camera as bridging songs between the scenes of the play. It was always intended that these would be recorded on a special day in the studio with Bowie simply playing to camera. He was accompanied on some of them by Dominic Muldowney, who was the musical director, but on many of them he was accompanying himself.

"Anyway, there was a drill. At times of high tension when broadcasting and really serious drama is taking place in the BBC, somewhere, somebody in the building will start a pneumatic drill. This happened intermittently through the morning and we had great difficulty in tracking down where this was coming from. Poor David was down in the studio during this time singing and every time it was, 'Cut, we can't complete'. He couldn't necessarily hear but we could and the mikes were picking up the reverberation from the drilling and it was ruining every single take. He was exhausted after all the work he'd been doing over the last four days in the studio, but we had to say, 'David, do you mind going on again?'

"There was a wonderful point when I actually went out myself and prowled around the building and found this guy with a pneumatic drill and personally told him to leave the building. It was quite extraordinary. In the end we had a set-to and he chucked his pneumatic drill on the floor and left the building.

"It was now about lunchtime so we decided that everything we had recorded in the morning was useless and we'd have to start all over again in the afternoon. David was wonderful. He was wearing the boots which he had to wear for the part, which were very tight for him, so his feet were killing him. He was on his feet the whole time. He didn't sit down for any of these songs — he was standing and performing straight to camera. He delivered better and better and better. It really was amazing to see this guy who had every reason to walk out of the studio and say he wasn't working in these conditions — but he didn't and we got some really wonderful material from him on that day."

THE BEAT GOES ON

S I X

Calm and collected. ▶

With the success of The Elephant Man and the filming of the Bertolt Brecht play Baal behind him, David was to embark on his third major film, The Hunger, in which he starred with Catherine Deneuve. His career was now veering towards filming. It was 1982 and, in fact, before the end of the year, work had commenced on his fourth feature film, Merry Christmas Mr Lawrence, which was directed by the controversial Japanese director, Nagisa Oshima and starred English actor Tom Conte, who along with Bowie, played a prisoner of war in Java.

By the end of the year, David had begun recording a new album in New York and it wasn't long before he was to sign a five year contract with EMI America, and release the 'Let's Dance' album which was produced by Nile Rogers.

Nile Rogers: "We met a few months before recording the 'Let's Dance' album. It was one night at an after-hours club because they're the hot spots in New York because no-one goes out until 2 or 3 in the morning. We were just babbling one night and going on about history of music and the whole bit, and I guess I made somewhat of an impression on him because he called me a few weeks later to work with him on his new album. I never dreamed in a million years that anything like that would happen because if you know anything about the music business, that's what we all do. It was remarkable that that turned into us actually working together from that chance meeting.

"I first got into David with the Ziggy Stardust album and then I went backwards and got into his earlier work. I remember I was living at Miami Beach at the time and I heard it pumping on the radio one day, and I couldn't believe what I heard. I was totally impressed. After that, when I got to England, I heard 'Rebel Rebel' and some other stuff, and it was then that I got totally into his work. When I got to see his look and his image and the whole thing, then I got totally into it. It was just exciting. There just wasn't anyone around like that then. He was an incredibly visual artist at the time.

"The interesting thing is we kept missing each other in the beginning because he was trying to call me and I totally didn't believe that this was happening, so I got all these messages around town that David Bowie had called and I thought it was different friends playing tricks on me because I had told them of our encounter from a few nights earlier, and I thought that they thought that this was the best joke in the world; so actually, we missed each other for weeks. Anyway, after we finally did meet and we decided that musically a collaboration between the two of us would make sense. He went over to Switzerland I guess and started working on some music and then he rang me and asked me to come

over and just listen to them and do demos of the songs together and these demos would be the basis of the album, which is exactly what we did. The thing with me is that I always treat demos as demos because you never know what's going to happen with the record once you start playing the music yourself. The interesting thing about David is his demos - he was just doing them right there in his house on a 12 string guitar and a simple tape recorder, so basically they sounded awful to me but that's OK because that's what I always expect demos to sound like. I think that the reason that this particular marriage worked so well is because we were able to work together right from the beginning. It was almost as if we developed them together because when I heard it, it was just one person singing on a guitar, so I feel my contribution was evident right from the beginning as I even did the demos with him, and even though our demos were fairly laughable, I just knew that when we got back to the States and we got the normal musicians that I liked to work with that it would be terrific. I kept saying to him, 'David don't worry, when we get home this is going to be fantastic,' and it was a very easy, relaxing project. I didn't have one problem from the word 'go' and I knew when eventually we made the record it would be terrific. We made it at the Power Station in New York City and we had various musicians including Omar Hakim, Tony Thompson, Carmine Rojas on bass, and we recorded it in 21 days. In fact, I believe we finished it in 19 days because I didn't come to work the last two days and I said to David, 'To me it sounds finished,' and he said 'No, no, no, we still have a little more work to do.' In fact we didn't really - it was done. They may have done some editing or fiddling around with it when I wasn't there, but I just remember coming in for about half an hour and he was having a sort of 'listening party' because the record wasn't signed and David did that independently. We just did it on our own and then he made the deal afterwards.

"When David first contacted me, he said, 'This is what we're going to do - it's a special project - we're out to make a record that people would like.' I thought that he wanted me to do 'Scary Monsters And Super Creeps Part II', which is in fact what I wanted to do, and I was quite shocked when he said, 'Nile, I want you to do a really great groove record with me,' and it did take a while for that to sink in, but once I understood we just did it. It was great because when I look back on the project I don't remember having any major confrontations other than things like what food we would eat and who's going to pay for it and things like that. Musically we seemed totally in 'sync'; it just all seemed to work and we were able to take these ideas and just

transform them into solid musical statements. At least that's how I looked at it anyway. I'm sure that the reason it worked so well was that the chemistry was exactly right. That means we didn't have to second guess ourselves. As we did it, we knew it was right and that was it. We didn't have to sit around and argue or contemplate on whether we were making important statements or whether the universe was shrinking or things like that. We just knew we were saying what we were supposed to say and it was right, and the fact that he was sure made me sure. Usually when the artist is a bit undecisive then it makes the producer a bit worried, but we'd finish something and David would say 'That's it, it's great,' and I'd say 'Fantastic, I was thinking the same thing.' We didn't toil over things. Sometimes people think that it makes the art less credible, but I think exactly the opposite; I think that when you're doing it and it's right, and you know it's right, then it's even more valid than if you toiled over it because you didn't know what you were doing; you somehow couldn't make up your mind and say 'This is really what I wanted to say.'

"I must say that when I met him, it was a time in my life when I was incredibly impressionable, so to have someone who was a hero of yours and you're working with them, it was like a vacuum cleaner - I sucked up all this information. I was incredibly taken by him - I was very, very impressed. He made me feel comfortable. I really had a good time working with him and I never felt that he was looking down on me or anything like that; I felt as if I was a peer or an equal and a collaborator and a partner for the project. When we started working, I had no idea how impressed I actually was going to be once we started working because when I work I'm incredibly confident. I give a lot to my job, I love doing this, and I was completely engrossed in my work. I guess maybe that's a little unfortunate but I really do love doing this, so I guess the by-product of that is that when I'm doing it I feel I'm really in my element and I feel quite comfortable and the fact that we felt so comfortable together right away just made me respect him more because a lot of times, people get fairly intimidated because when they come around to this situation - we have all the technology, we know what we're doing, all the musicians are really good players and I like to

The joke is on Dylan. ▶

5 years on – Serious Moonlight '83. ▶

have good staff, good engineers - it's you against me. It's like here's my team with all my people and it's just you all by yourself - it's got to be intimidating. But David got on with everyone right away and it was great."

Carlos Alomar: "After he signed with the new record company (EMI America), what happened was that he got a new audience. Those kids that were nine years old suddenly became 14/15 year olds - perfect album buying age. Suddenly 'Let's Dance' came out and he was a big hit. The immediate effect was his consciousness change. He wanted to get rid of the old - not only did he change his record company but he changed his total staff. He changed his office. He changed the name of his office and his corporation. He changed his whole touring situation. Everything except me and the chauffeur and the tour manager, Eric Barrett.

"You see, I can change. I study different types of music and play any type of music. I've always been able to change no matter where he wanted to go, and that's been good. Second reason is that I'm the only one who knows all the material back to the 70's so I'm able to teach the material to anybody. I orchestrate. I'm like a band leader, so no matter whether he gives me 14 pieces, 18 pieces, 2 pieces or 7 pieces, I can still orchestrate for them and I have the ability to take the music that he wants to orchestrate and do it differently, but he won't have to change the way he sings. In fact, I did the whole Serious Moonlight tour; getting all the music together, the segues, the orchestration and some of the horn arrangements, vocal arrangements, choreography and things like that. So he feels very comfortable to just say 'Carlos, take care of this and that' and then I go in and take care of all the parts. I even sing his part and get everybody ready. When the whole show is ready to go, he comes in and does it and he doesn't have to worry about the show. All he has to do is come in and sing. Even if the arrangements are changed, he studies the same things. He can study his old records at home. His vocal will still be the same although the music around it will have changed.

"The first thing we did together was 'Fame' with John Lennon. There was Lennon, Bowie and myself. I was playing a lick or something, or a line, or something that he liked and that's where we started with 'Fame'. It used to be 'Footstompin', a rock and roll song. Anyway, he liked what I was playing but he wouldn't like the song so he'd change it and cut it up until finally it became 'Fame'. Then I

overdubbed 4 or 5 guitar parts and he liked that. After that we did 'Station to Station' and that was more rock and roll.

"Musically he's quite good as far as getting ideas. His selection and choice are excellent. You see, you have to have a very good knack for picking and selecting people you want to work together. It can be a catastrophy or a blessing. If you pick the wrong people, they're not going to give you anything. When I work with David, the musicians that he gives me, I always make sure that they come through the way they are. I don't tell them what to play, just direct them towards the music. He has a great knack of selecting the right musicians to work with each other. He's had some great lead guitarists, great keyboard players and all that, always; not to mention a wonderful rhythm guitarist like me!

"His writing is amazing. His words are fantastic. The musical part of it - it's all right but it doesn't kill me, partly because I am to blame and that's what he wants. But the writing is excellent and it comes in scattered bits. He has many different methods to construct a lyric which is rather nice because you don't get blocked. They come in free verse or they can come in cutting up little notes to himself and putting them all together, free rhyme - anything but a limerick. He's very good as far as the function of writing a song is concerned, and quite fast too. Extremely so, especially when he's doing an album. He won't let up until it's done. It's all you think about when you're doing an album - nothing else. Twenty-four hours - you dream it, sleep it and eat it. When we first started doing albums, he was used to two or three months with the Spiders from Mars and stuff like that, but when we did the first album, 'Young Americans', that took four weeks to record the rhythm section and probably another week or two to mix, so that's a month. Since 1974 he hasn't done an album in more than two months. Usually an album is completed in two months which is extremely fast. In fact, very, very fast. Once the ideas start flowing, he doesn't want to block it by taking too much time off - only for the mix do you really take off any time - and the actual construction of the songs and putting them down should only take two or three weeks, but mixing it, that can take forever. Some bands will take three or four months just to mix."

Bowie's 1983 Serious Moonlight tour opened in June at Wembley Arena in London from where it moved to Birmingham and Milton Keynes. Every show was a sell-out within a day of announcement.

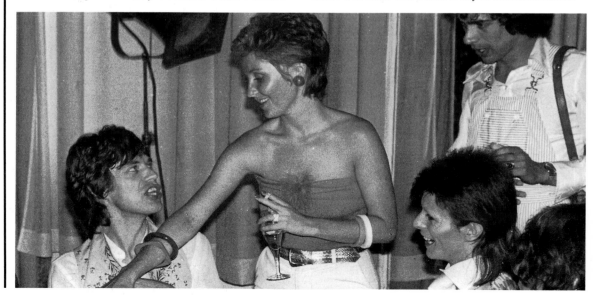

Jagger, Lulu, Bowie & Warren Peace – gassing at the Cafe Royal. ▶

The promoter was quoted as saying that it was easily the biggest response to any show he had previously handled, out selling the outstanding success of the Rolling Stones shows of the previous year, and all this in spite of the fact that Bowie had been out of the public eye for a considerable period of time. It wasn't long, however, until he was back in front of the cameras again.

For the Far Eastern leg of the Serious Moonlight tour, Bowie decided to take along his own film crew to record events, documentary fashion. Produced by Bhaskar Bhattachoryia, the film became 'Ricochet' and was released shortly after the completion of the tour.

Bhaskar Bhattachoryia: "David was coming to the end of his Serious Moonlight tour which covered Europe and America and was hugely successful and of course, all of those concerts had been videoed. But he also decided to go to Hong Kong, Bangkok, Singapore and Kuala Lumpur after Japan, Australia and New Zealand. As far as his management were concerned, they weren't very enthusiastic about doing the countries in South East Asia, partly because there wouldn't be an audience like there would in the rest of the world, so they decided to call it a 'Bungle in the jungle'.

"David, however, was determined to go to South East Asia to explore new territory and new audiences. He also wanted a visual record of that tour. What he didn't want was the normal rock and roll tour story - the boys in the backroom, the roadies, endless hotel rooms and everything which normally went with such events. He wanted something more of a 'travelogue' in the BBC genre where a presenter - a traveller - goes to different

countries and has all sorts of experiences and meets local people; as a result he wanted a director who was not really from the rock and roll business. His agents and PR scouted around and finally suggested that they should talk to Jerry Troiner, who had directed two of the great railway and river journeys for the BBC. Troiner, a very respected documentary film maker went to see Bowie at the Savoy.

"After the meeting, Jerry decided to do the film and shortly after work started in the Far East. We had about two weeks to do the recce and about ten days to shoot the film in three countries, Hong Kong, Bangkok, and Singapore. Kuala Lumpur didn't come off and thank God it didn't because it would have killed us and killed the band as well. It didn't work out because of the Malaysian government's bureaucracy.

"We had sequences in Bangkok where he'd go into the middle of nowhere where nobody knows him - he's just another white face around and you see the sequence in which an exorcist spits water into his face, which has been misinterpreted as 'the man spat on him', but it was really a blessing because he went to an exorcist and sought his blessing so that his future travel would be graced.

"Naturally, every day was an adventure, but the one that I suppose sticks in my mind was when we'd started at 3.00 in the morning one day to go up the Klong, a local waterway in Bangkok. There had been severe floods in Bangkok that year and we all went off at 3.00 in the morning in boats in the darkness, and we filmed all day in Buddhist monasteries, musicians' places, with an exorcist, teashops - in fact, all over the place. David went round, rolled up his trousers and walked through the

▲
Bowie and Cher on the 'Cher Show' '75.

Over page: Around the world with Bowie. ►►

RTL
présente

DAVID BOWIE
en concert

PARIS
les 24 et 25 Mai
...illon de Paris

LYON
le 26 Mai
au Palais des Sports

MARSEILLE
le 27 Mai
au Parc Chaneau

EMPIRE POOL, WEMBLEY

M.A.M./John Smith Entertainments/
Earley Associates presents

DAVID BOWIE
ON STAGE

SATURDAY, 8 MAY, 1976
at 8 p.m.

SOUTH GRAND TIER
£3.75

TO BE RETAINED See conditions on back

MAY
8

ENTER AT
SOUTH DOOR
ENTRANCE

75
ROW
B
SEAT
106

David Bo...
Konserten flyttad
till Kungl. Tennishallen!

Köpta biljetter inlöses torsdag 25/5
hos Svala och Söderlund,
Kungsgatan 43.

Ny... ...& fredan 26/5 hos S och S.

BOWIE SYSTE...
ボウイーの音楽的...

David Bowie
...IVE ON STAGE
WITH SPECIAL GUESTS
THE ANGELS'

DAVID BOWIE'S NEW ALBUM 'STAGE'
NOW AVAILABLE ON RCA RECORDS & TAPES

R.A.S. of N.S.W. — SHOWGROUND
FRIDAY, NOVEMBER 24, 19...
Tickets: $12.5...

Bookings: Hord...
Mitchells/...
Bran...

MITCHELLS BASS
COMPUTER BOX OFFICES
Computicket

PAUL DAINTY PRESENTS

David Bowie

N° 446

LIVE ON STAGE
...CIAL GUESTS THE ANGELS

...YDNEY SHOWGROUND
...Y, 24th NOVEMBER, 1978
at 7.30 p.m.

...(Subject to conditions on back of ticket)

WE PLAY RAIN OR SHINE

DAVID BOW...

Fred. 2 jun...

Blj. Svala & Söderlund...
Best Ivan Brand...

A M
A JEREMY...

malaria-ridden water like we all did. We had a wonderful day filming and it was one of those days when we had no pressure, no superstar pressure on him and he didn't have to behave like a superstar. He could just be one of the boys and enjoy himself and eat off the floating markets.

"After that long day's filming, from 3.00 in the morning, we came back at about 11.00 p.m. that night, so it was something like twenty hours on the road with no sleep, and it was very hard work. Now, it just so happened that it was the King's birthday, and on the King's birthday in Bangkok, everything

shuts because it's the festive season. There are millions of people out on the streets and hundreds of movies being shown, and it was just impossible to move. When we came back, his car wasn't there waiting for him (because he's used to having a limo waiting for him to take him back to the hotel but this day there was none), so he, CoCo, his personal assistant, his photographer Denis O'Regan and one of the production assistants Kim, had to look for a taxi, but they couldn't find one. All they could find was one of those scooter taxis which are really meant for two people, but they did manage to get four people into the two-seater, and the superstar and the others got in there on their knees and went through the crowd. I think it took them an hour for a 10 minute journey but they reached the hotel at about midnight, totally exhausted, straw in hair, trousers rolled up, looking like dishevelled tramps, and there were the fans waiting for him, naturally expecting a huge limo to roll up. But this little tut-tut chugged along and out of it poured these four dishevelled people including David Bowie. He immediately ran into the hotel. I dare say he was exhausted, had a headache and was just not interested in signing autographs that evening.

"The music clips in the finished film were of the concerts. I remember he did one concert in Bangkok, one in Singapore and two in Hong Kong. And, in fact, he did a very moving tribute to John Lennon on December 8. That was the last show of the Serious Moonlight tour in Hong Kong and was the anniversary of John Lennon's death. He sang 'Imagine' to the Hong Kong audience and it was a very moving experience because I think he was very

Bowie Tonight. ▶▶

moved. To me, it was the most enthusiastic applause he received on the whole tour.

"I think the whole project came about because he did spend some time with the Noh Theatre, and was involved with Lindsay Kemp and the Noh Theatre's roots in Japanese Buddhism. He also spent some time, although I don't know how long, at a Buddhist monastery in Scotland."

Mary Finnigan: "It was back in the 60's that David first became involved in Buddhism. He was wandering around London when he wandered into the Buddhist Centre and instead of going into the main reception area, went down into the library where he met Chimi Rimpoche, who was a Tibetan lama and it's rumoured at that point that he seriously considered becoming a Buddhist monk although I feel that because he had to make a choice between showbusiness and the life in a monastery, which is very strict and all time consuming, he settled for the show business.

"A year or so later when he was living with me in Beckenham and we were running the Arts Lab, we used to have musical evenings and on a couple of evenings, Chimi Rimpoche came down to give talks on Buddhism. I believe that David is still in touch with Chimi to this day."

Bhaskar Bhattachoryia: "I dare say that a lot of people who went through the 60's and 70's, for whatever reason, let's just say for extended consciousness and experiments with extended consciousness, found themselves involved in an alternative way of looking at the world, and I suppose the Buddhist metaphysics explained, or rather rationalized, their various experiences with other states of consciousness, and I suppose the roots of it are there. Although this is a guess, because a lot of people at that time found themselves more attuned to Buddhist explanation of the mind rather than a Christian explanation of morality.

"But going back to the film Ricochet, I don't think David wanted to stick to the little white world. He wanted to try and reach out to a wider audience and I think it works both ways because I'm sure he absorbs part of their culture within himself. Whether it actually comes out in the music is another matter, but I think it's affected him because he spent time in Bali and considerable time in Japan. As far as the politics are concerned, say in a place like Thailand as you see in the film Ricochet, it's a country that's been exploited to an incredibly horrific degree. Bangkok was where the soldiers went to do their RNR and Bangkok is still full of westerners who just go there on their annual sex leave. Again, we show this in the film, and this is a point he wanted to make, that this was exploitation of war in South East Asia and more subtle forms of exploitation like the sexual exploitation that is going on now is not really that different. They are both forms of imperialism of one sort or another. I think you're bound to have contradictions and I prefer to think of them as paradoxes, maybe they wouldn't have any art. The fact that you can actually see a Van Gogh painting and it can send you into the heights of ecstasy and you feel really good seeing that painting, doesn't mean that the man didn't suffer.

"The Serious Moonlight tour had taken eight months and the managers and everyone were very tired. They're not artists, they're business people and they could say 'All right, let's make cents,' but David I think wanted to do the film for artistic reasons as well as for business. It's like that with any agent or manager who manages an artist. They

David Bowie
in japan

追跡取材 デヴィッド・ボウイーが日本で見せた素顔

研ぎ澄まれた感性が今、海を超えた

某酒造メーカーのコマーシャルでお茶の間に登場したデヴィッド・ボウイー。その世界は、僕らが失いかけていた日本人の持つ鋭くしなやかな精神を呼び起こしてくれる。根っから日本好きという彼は、滞在中、数々のエピソードによって彼の秘められた人間性を示してくれた。

● 若林 茂 (本誌)

PIC. MASAYOSHI SUKITA

treat their artists often like little children - 'Oh no, he's having another whim again' – and they've got to curb it before he goes off on another tangent. But David actually insisted on it, and thank God he did because I think, at the end of the day, he will be proved right; that he followed his instincts rather than listen to pure commercial sense. It was shortly after completing the film that he went on to make the album 'Tonight'."

Hugh Padgham: "We talked about where we were going to record it and it wasn't going to be in North America or in England, presumably for tax reasons, and we didn't want to go to Compass Point studios in Nassau because Jagger was doing his solo album there and we thought it would be a bit uncool if he was in the studio next to us. So I came up with a studio in Canada near Montreal, called Morian Heights, which is a very good studio and one that I had been to once before with The Police. The useful part about it is that it's only an hour to the airport and an hour to New York and most of the musicians were based in New York, so I thought it was a good idea. Eventually we decided to do it there and everyone hated me by the end of the album because it's right in the middle of nowhere and there's nothing to do, but because we did the album pretty quickly it didn't worry me because I was always busy, but if you're a musician and you've done your bit, you've obviously got time to hang out and there's nothing to do except watch videos and walk in the forest and things. It is great in the winter because you can ski, being a skiing resort, and the reason we were there with The Police was because they enjoy skiing, but this was May, just after the snow had gone.

"We had Omar Hakim on drums, Carlos Alomar on guitar, who also works as the musical director for the band, Carmine Rojas who was on bass, and keyboards were really done by David and Derek who was producing. Derek was really a bass player but between the two of them they could sort of fiddle around on the keyboard. That was the main line up. The horn section was the one that he'd used on 'Let's Dance'.

"David had already done some demos in Switzerland with Derek over a period of a few days or a week or something, so they had pretty well most of the songs anyway, although some of the songs came together in the studio - they were just called '1','2','3' I think - more or less writing on mike, but the majority of songs they'd worked out and they actually had pretty good demos. They used a local drummer in Switzerland for those. I must admit I was quite impressed actually with the demos and thought 'why are they bothering to go back in the studio again?' It was pretty well organized, but it had to be to do an album in five and a half weeks. I was really drafted in as an engineer because Derek was producing and I ended up with co-production credit just because I can't help but put my oar in. That's what I do all the time.

"I remember one night we were doing 'Dancing With The Big Boys' and we just stayed up all night with David and Iggy Pop in the studio and a few bottles of lager, just writing the lyrics as they went along. It was good fun because Iggy's a good bloke - his mind is definitely somewhere else - and he wasn't like anything I imagined him to be. He was very quiet. Everything went pretty smoothly as we were just there to work and certainly there wasn't an enormous amount of looning about. Everything was very good-natured and the musicians, Carmine, Carlos and Omar, were just so incredible, you could just see the music flowing out of their bodies as they put down the backing tracks very quickly. Omar, who was on drums, would play the song through once and the next take we'd probably record it. It was amazing. And it was good doing vocals with David and Iggy just coming out with anything they came out with. We'd stop, look at it and wind back and do a little bit again or something, and I was just recording them on their own tracks. I think most people's conception of him (Iggy) is being a

At work in '75. ▲

complete lunatic who is just out to lunch and running around like a madman all the time. When he came in, he had these big glasses on and he just used to sit in the control room and read. My idea of Iggy now is that of an intellectual because it's the only time I've met Iggy so I really don't know what he was like before. I presume he's been through crazier times - I guess we all mellow.

"Because the studio was in the middle of nowhere, we had to get someone to come in and cook for us every evening. Because it's a skiing resort, there's a little town about five miles down the road called Morian Heights with about 6,000 inhabitants and about 60 restaurants as it's in French Canada and they're really into food. We got this cook from one of the restaurants who was a friend of the studio to come up, and he used to cook this unbelievable food. Every night, the high point of the day was going back to the house, which was about half a mile away from the studio, and we just used to sit around a table and eat and have great chats. Everybody was really friendly and we just had a good laugh. Iggy was there probably for about three weeks.

"When I first arrived I was just sort of the engineer. It hadn't really been discussed that much. I hadn't met David before we got into the studio and he arrived the day after me. I feel he had a pretty good idea of how he wanted it to turn out because he'd recorded some pretty good demos, so it was just a question of having a listen to the demo and then going in and doing it. There was very little deliberation or discussion of how things should go - he'd got all that together. I think this is because he works with good people who know what they're doing. He's worked with Carlos for years and years."

Carlos Alomar: "Our working relationship was just based on my musical ability. I'd get together with the drummer or the bass player and we'd work out a song – maybe reggae, slow, fast or up-tempo. We'd let David hear it three or four different ways and whichever way he wanted to do it, then we just did it. So our relationship was based on our mutual dependence. He throws out what he wants to hear

and then I give it back to him. If he doesn't like it, there's always an endless selection of other ways to do it. That's the easiest way to work together. Even down to the last thing we did which was 'Dancing With The Big Boys' on the 'Tonight' album – that was just thrown out there. You know, he says 'How about something like this?' and I say 'OK, fine' and just start grooving and just start playing until you come up with something. That ability has been like the saving grace; just to throw something out there and just jam it up until it becomes a song. It's very difficult to do and that's something that he likes. That's how we used to do all the old demos and get together with some people and make demos, but before, everything we did was constructed, thought of, written, conceived, everything in the studio just working with nothing."

Hugh Padgham: "David was an amazing singer. A lot of singers that I work with are very nervous about it. It's a sort of 'Oh, I've got to do the vocals now and I might take a few hours to do a vocal.' But David would go in and sing about a verse for you to get a level on the mike and then he'd sing it twice at the most, and that was the vocal done - he was absolutely incredible. So professional that it just knocked me out. He'd just go in there and sing it, about five minutes later, there was your vocal. It was great. And you can see why he doesn't take long to do albums. There's no messing about, he just does the job."

Carlos Alomar: "There was a time when David used to say, 'Look I'm going to change the music, I'm going to change the song and the way I'm going to do it is by getting rid of Carlos.' It was in the papers and everything. Then the tour would come up and he couldn't do it in the time that he'd given himself so he called me back to do it. When he feels strong enough just to go out there by himself without me, then it will be over. I've given 14 years now, so how much more I'm supposed to get out of the thing, I don't know. I'm basically a musician. That's why of late I've been working with other people. I co-wrote Mick Jagger's solo album 'She's the Boss', and Debbie Harry's album, 'She's Coming Back', and I've done a lot of other solo projects this year with other named musicians, like Paul McCartney's new album, and the fact that I've made myself available has actually allowed me to work more.

"The thing is that with David I have my position and it's a good position filled with responsibility, but once the time comes then I'd rather just keep it neat. He certainly doesn't owe me anything. I've done faithful work and he's been pretty faithful but the situation is that everybody thinks three things: that I work exclusively with David; that I'm much too expensive because I work with Bowie; or that they don't know how to reach me or they don't know where I live or things like that. Under this situation, everybody would think I'm almost always with David. So, in the last year and a half I figured, 'Let me just start working with some other people and let the world know that it's not that way.' It's comfortable, but it's unnecessary for me to be exclusive to David. I'm able to get around and play with other musicians which has been pretty good."

Angie Bowie: "It was towards the end of recording the 'Tonight' album, or somewhere around that time, that David's step-brother Terry committed suicide. Terry, by definition, I believe was classified as a schizophrenic. In fact, he lived in my house for about six months when we were living back in Beckenham in the early 70's, and I looked after him. At that time I did try to wean him away from the

JAZZIN' FOR BLUE JEAN

drugs which were prescribed. There was part of me, basically an uneducated part - a person not that well equipped, that was frightened. I didn't know if I was doing the right thing, I really didn't. I hadn't seen 'One Flew Over the Cuckoo's Nest' and didn't know about electric shock treatment, although I did know that I certainly wouldn't like to have had it because he'd been subjected to all these indignities and I just tended him and treated him like a special guest and spent time with him and just chatted away. He was a very well read man and a very interesting man, but with the drugs that were prescribed by Cane Hill Hospital for him, he would tend to really not talk too much so we would talk in the morning, I guess before he would feel the necessity to take whatever the medication was. I think with David, he attempted to be up-front about the fact that his brother was unwell and it was an excuse for himself later during drug-induced paranoia. He adored

Blue Jean bizarre.

Serious in Japan. ▶

Terry and always had the highest respect for him. He really loved him and always had a very good relationship with him.

"I think there is also the regret, or the guilt, that taking the time and trouble, private care as opposed to the National Health care, could have cured him. I think David knew exactly what had to be done and I don't think he felt he had the time or that he could take the time off from working as hard as he worked at his career to be able to support it, because basically David's mother had never been able to deal with Terry's illness, and his auntie Pat couldn't deal with it either. So, in the end, he was just packed off to a National Health mental institute and, sadly, that didn't solve anything. Sometimes people just throw their hands up. When all the stories in the press appeared about David not attending Terry's funeral, I don't think it was a case of David didn't want to go. I don't think he didn't want to do something about it. He just looked at the problem

and realized the magnitude of it. It was so enormous that to have got involved he really would have been working on a voluntary basis taking care of someone who had already been abused by the system from far too young an age when David was too young to have been able to do anything about it. I think if you have a real zest and an ambition to do something, or to demonstrate a talent, it's worse, because you do get caught up in yourself and wrapped up 24 hours a day working at what you want to do."

Tony Visconti: "I met his brother when I went down to Haddon Hall when he was living with Angie in Beckenham. I just used to go down and see his mum and see how he was doing and his brother would often be there at weekends because he was an out-patient, or he would have weekends out of the mental institution that he was in at the time."

The Sun: "Rock idol, David Bowie, was lashed by his aunt today for snubbing his half-brother's funeral. Grief stricken Pat hit out at the millionaire

122

singer saying 'I hope God forgives you David - this is a tragic rejection.' Bowie stayed at his house in Switzerland while Terry was cremated near his mother's home in Kent. Terry, 47, died after falling in front of a train earlier this month. He's been treated in hospital for schizophrenia. Bowie sent a wreath to the funeral with the inscription: 'You've seen more things than we can imagine, but all these moments will be lost like tears washed away by the rain. God bless you. David."

Angie Bowie: "I think Terry and Lindsay Kemp were both joint influences on David's life. They introduced him to the original New York poets like Kerouac and both Terry and Lindsay talked to David about these people and made them come alive for David as influences and people who had something important to say."

Lindsay Kemp: "I wanted him to be a total artist which, in fact, he is. I always encouraged him to paint and to draw. He'd already studied painting and drawing but I think I helped make him make more of himself."

With the completion of the film Ricochet which was released on Virgin video, and the album 'Tonight', Bowie's film career continues with two films completed this year (1986), 'Labyrinth', the Jim Henson/George Lucas film, and 'Absolute Beginners', which was directed by Julien Temple.

Julien Temple: "We consciously tried to echo his real life myth with the myth in the film. He is, in a sense, the pied piper who leads successive movements across an incredibly long period of time, or certainly in pop culture anyway. He is an amazing chameleon character and we did very much want to bring that understanding to the part.

"We were excited to make this film not just as a nostalgic return to '58, but very much contrasting and comparing '58 with '85. David's humorous playing in it is very strong. For a long time he had a very serious, almost mystical presentation of himself, and I think the recent things that he's done have shown that very interesting side of him that was not there before. He's got the confidence to be more humorous and explore his own mythology."

Angie Bowie: "I think that David was able to achieve what he wanted to achieve through his own dynamic approach to things. This was due to his ruthlessness which included weeding out anyone who did not contribute to his own dream of what he wanted his artistry to encapture."

Carlos Alomar: "We're talking about somebody who knows what he wants to do in everything - it's pretty calculated. I don't mean to make it sound cold, it's just that there are reasons for everything and he's looking for reasons. I would describe David as being a little calculating. He's as sincere as possible when you get into the mega-superstar bit, but all of that is just based on who you can use and who you can't."

Angie Bowie: "I think he's accomplished what he set out to do, and one's contribution to that success is what is satisfying about the David Bowie mystique and aura."

Carlos Alomar: "In '74 'Fame' came out, and that was the first time he had bridged going to AM - he was always FM. At that point everybody was just watching in awe as mystique and everything took off."

◄
From '75 to '83 – the Bowie magic continues.
◄

From Labyrinth 1986. ▶

Off Duty. ▶▶

Angie Bowie: "The Band Aid example, and that entire vehicle of causing some good to be done, is an area where I am sure he will make his influence felt. He feels very strongly about the fate of children, the fate of people who are less privileged than he is, due to his father's working for so long as PR with Dr Barnardo's. I think that influenced him as a young man and as a performing artist when he used to go there and do shows for them. I think that will probably come to the forefront.

"Basically, he lives very much in areas of artistry where the person is unobtainable because that's a relationship that he doesn't have to give anything to. He can just suck from their books, their paintings, their work, something which fulfills him. He doesn't need to give anything back. What he gives back is to his audience; his ability to categorise something and make it something different and David Bowie."

A Who's Who of 'In Other Words David Bowie'

Angie Bowie: David Bowie's former wife who met and fell in love with David when she was 19. She became an intrinsic part of his life in the days when he was a struggling musician through to his rise to fame. Angela Barnet, born in 1950 in Cyprus where her family lived, the daughter of an American George Barnet (whose parentage was English) and Helen Marie (who came from Poland), was educated in America and Europe and ultimately in Kingston Polytechnic in London. She married David in March, 1970 and had one son, Zowie who was born on 28th May, 1971. David and Angela's divorce became final on 8th February 1980.

Julien Temple: Director of the film 'Absolute Beginners' (1986). Temple first came to the public eye in 1977 when he directed a Sex Pistols film 'The Great Rock and Roll Swindle'.
He has also made many rock promo videos including 'Blue Jean' for Bowie and the controversial 'Undercover' for The Rolling Stones. His more recent work was on a feature length film 'Running Out Of Luck' which starred Mick Jagger.

Hugh Padgham: Record Producer who has been involved with Phil Collins and Adam Ant and more recently Tears For Fears. Padgham was joint producer of the Bowie 'Tonight' album.

Nile Rogers: Record Producer who has worked with Chic and produced the David Bowie album 'Let's Dance' (1983).

Tony Visconti: Has been both a friend and a record producer for David from the 60's through to the 80's. Visconti produced the second Bowie album 'David Bowie' (1969) and went on to produce: 'The Man Who Sold The World' (1971), 'David Live' (1974), 'Young Americans' (1975), 'Low' (1977), "Heroes" (1978), 'Stage' (1978), 'Lodger' (1979) and 'Scary Monsters And Super Creeps' (1980).
He was also involved in the 'Diamond Dogs' album (1974) and remains a friend of David's to this day. Tony Visconti has just completed nine months work on a Moody Blues album and runs his own studio in central London.

Brian Eno: Left the successful Roxy Music in 1972 and began solo work on pure electronic music. Worked with Bowie on the controversial 'Low' in 1976 and went on to make "Heroes" and 'Lodger', completing a trilogy of albums with Bowie. Eno has been a pioneer of ambient music and produced albums for Talking Heads, collaborating with David Byrne, and U2. More recently, his work with Russell Mills has culminated in a book on both artists' work entitled 'More Dark Than Shark'.

Carlos Alomar: Has worked with David as a guitarist and band leader since the mid 70's and has been involved in the albums:
'Diamond Dogs' (1974), 'Young Americans' (1975), 'Station to Station' (1976), 'Low' (1977), "Heroes" (1978), 'Stage' (1978), 'Lodger' (1979), 'Scary Monsters And Super Creeps' (1980).
Carlos first worked with David in the studio but then joined him for the 1976 World Tour. From then on he became David's band leader, organizing the musicians through to the Serious Moonlight Tour of 1983.

Jack Hofsiss: Director of 'The Elephant Man' in which Bowie played the leading role of John Merrick. The production opened on Broadway in September, 1980 and ran till January 1981.

Anthony Zanetta: Former President of MainMan, the company set up by Tony DeFries to handle David Bowie's affairs after he parted with Ken Pitt. Tony Zanetta was also David's personal assistant during the early 1970s.

Julie Weiss: Make-up artist for the Broadway production of The Elephant Man.

Louis Marks: Producer of the Bertolt Brecht play 'Baal', produced for BBC Television and broadcast in March, 1982. David Bowie played the lead role of Baal.

Bhaskar Bhattachoryia: Producer of the film 'Ricochet' (1984) which was christened 'Bungle In The Jungle' by David's management. The film was mainly shot in South East Asia and was financed by Bowie's own company. It also included footage from his eight month Serious Moonlight Tour of 1983.

Nicolas Roeg: English film director who directed Bowie's first major film, 'The Man Who Fell To Earth', which was released in the UK in 1976. Roeg also produced 'Performance' which starred Mick Jagger, and his other films include 'Don't Look Now', 'Walkabout', 'Bad Timing', 'Eureka' and 'Insignificance'.

Leee Childers: Former photographer with MainMan. Both Anthony Zanetta and Leee Childers met David when playing in the cast of Pork, an Andy Warhol production staged in London during 1971.

Sean Mayes: Keyboard player on the 1978 World Tour who came to Bowie's attention when playing in Fumble, a rock and roll band who supported David in 1972. Mayes kept a diary of the entire tour from which his book 'We Can Be Heroes' was compiled. It is due to be published soon.

Mick Ronson: Guitarist who played with David's band in the early 70's and toured America with Ziggy Stardust as one of 'The Spiders From Mars'. Ronson also played on: 'The Man Who Sold The World' (1971), 'Hunky Dory' (1971), 'The Rise And Fall Of Ziggy Stardust And The Spiders From Mars' (1972), 'Aladdin Sane' (1973), 'Pin-ups' (1973).

Ronson has also played with Ian Hunter, Mott The Hoople, Sandy Dillon and Bob Dylan.

Lindsay Kemp: Film producer, painter, poet, classical writer and mime artiste who studied under Marcel Marceau. Kemp has also appeared in films by Fellini and Cassavetes. It was Kemp who taught Bowie the art of mime and included him in Pierrot In Turquoise, a touring production staged by Kemp's company. Apart from appearances in 'Pierrot', Kemp later appeared alongside Bowie in a Ziggy Stardust show at The Rainbow Theatre in 1972. Kemp now lives in Italy where he stages regular productions and appears in various television shows.

Natasha Kornilof: A costume designer who made the costumes for Pierrot In Turquoise and also painted the scenery, with David Bowie, on the floor of her flat. Natasha has since become one of the most respected costume designers in show business, designing both for television and for the stage. She designed the costumes for David Bowie's 1978 World Tour, the clown costume that he wore on the single cover of 'Ashes To Ashes' as well as costumes for David's appearance on the American television programme Saturday Night Live in 1979/1980.

Brian Lane: One of David's teachers at Bromley Technical High School, where he still teaches today.

Vic Furlong: Owner of the music shop where David worked as a Saturday boy when he was at school. It was from Vic's shop that he bought his first "plastic" saxophone.

Roger Raven: Musician who played with 'Comos', the resident band at the arts lab in Bromley.

Mrs Margaret Jones: David's Mother. (Publication only)

Gus Dudgeon: Producer of 'Space Oddity' and recording engineer on the first 'David Bowie' album (1967). Gus was later to become Elton John's producer.

Mary Finnigan: A journalist with whom David Bowie lived in the late 60's and with whom David started a folk club which was to become an arts lab providing a stage for mime, theatre and the general development of art. Mary is now a radio journalist working with both the BBC and independent radio.

Ken Pitt: David's manager from the mid 60's through to 1970. Pitt became involved in the music business in the 50's and in the 60's managed Crispian St. Peters, Manfred Mann and The Kinks, his most recent involvements having been with Rod McKuen. Bowie's interest was broadened under Pitt's management and during this period, he made his first album and his first film which was financed by Pitt, a film from which the single 'Space Oddity' evolved.

Dana Gillespie: Childhood friend of David's who went on to become an artist in her own right as a singer and actress, and who played the lead role in the original production of Jesus Christ Superstar (Mary Magdalen). Their relationship started when she first saw David performing at the Marquee in London from where it was often said that he carried her ballet shoes home from school. It was a friendship that started in the early 60's through to the mid 70's. Dana Gillespie is now living in Vienna, still pursuing a career as a singer and actress.

George Underwood: First met David when he was in the Cubs at the age of nine. George became David's closest friend at school and they still remain friends to this day. Underwood played in some of the early groups with David. Although dropped out of the music business to become a commercial artist, he still accompanied David on his first Ziggy Stardust tour of America. George also designed the album sleeve for the second 'David Bowie' album (1969) and was also involved with the album sleeves for 'Ziggy Stardust' and 'Hunky Dory'.

Denis Taylor: Musician in The Lower Third, the band David Jones joined as a vocalist shortly after leaving Les Conn's management and The King Bees.

Les Conn: Les Conn arranged the first recording deal for David Jones (as he was then) and The King Bees and managed the group in 1964. He also managed Marc Bolan.

Ronnie Ross: Jazz saxophonist who gave Bowie his first lessons on the saxophone in 1970. Ross is still an active session musician.

Brian Lane: One of David's teachers at Bromley Technical High School, where he still teaches today.

Further reading

'The Pitt Report' Kenneth Pitt – Omnibus Press (1983)

'Ziggy Stardust (Bowie 1972/1973)' Mick Rock – St. Martin's Press (1984)

'Stardust' Tony Zanetta & Henry Edwards –Michael Joseph (1986)

'David Bowie – A Chronology' Kevin Cann – Vermilion (1983)

'Alias David Bowie' Peter & Leni Gillman – Hodder and Stoughton (1986)

'The Starzone Interviews' – Omnibus Press (1985)

'David Bowie – Illustrated Record' Roy Carr and Charles Shaar Murray – Eel Pie (1981)

'David Bowie Black Book' Miles – Omnibus Press (1980)